SESSIONS WITH JOHN & JUDE

Smyth & Helwys Publishing, Inc.
6316 Peake Road
Macon, Georgia 31210-3960
1-800-747-3016
© 2009 by Smyth & Helwys Publishing
All rights reserved.
Printed in the United States of America.

The paper used in this publication meets the minimum
requirements of American National Standard for Information
Sciences—Permanence of Paper for Printed Library Materials.

Library of Congress Cataloging-in-Publication Data

Qualls, Charles.

Sessions with John and Jude:
God's abiding words for an active faith / by Charles Qualls.
p. cm. Includes bibliographical references (p.) and index.
ISBN 978-1-57312-535-2 (pbk. : alk. paper)
1. Bible. N.T. Epistles of John—Textbooks. 2. Bible.
N.T. Jude—Textbooks. I. Title.
BS2805.55.Q36 2009 227'.940071—dc22 2009010527

Sessions *with*
John
• • • & Jude

God's Abiding *Words*
for an *Active Faith*

Charles Qualls

SMYTH&HELWYS
PUBLISHING INCORPORATED • MACON, GEORGIA

Acknowledgments

. . . to Peter Rhea Jones for kindling in me the interest to study 1, 2, and 3 John especially. His marvelous scholarship and pastor's heart make him a teacher to admire.

. . . the people of Second-Ponce de Leon Baptist Church, Atlanta, Georgia, have been a willing audience as we've "road-tested" most of these Scripture texts. Whether in devotionals, Bible studies, or sermons, they have worked with me to craft these sessions. Importantly, we have lived them out to each other on our best days.

. . . my friends at Smyth & Helwys are to be thanked because they grant me the grace to write. Keith Gammons was a friend before I ever published a thought. He has been my editor and encourager in the written word for some time now. Michael McCullar's vision brought about this handy series of studies. His skillful nurture of the books sees them into being.

. . . and of course, Elizabeth, without whose partnership nary a written syllable could come from me. You empower me to heed God's call, and you believe in me. For this I am eternally grateful; by this I am forever amazed. I can tell of God's love because you live it out before me each day.

Table of Contents

Preface

Sessions with John & Jude is designed for group Bible study. Each session brings to the teaching experience some background and group discussion questions. This is a starting place from which to build a teaching plan. The goal of this book is to provide an approachable overview of these largely ignored letters from the New Testament. Combined with current headlines and past experiences of church life, the user should be able to craft a helpful study time for his or her participants. Though shrouded in some mystery, these small writings shed important light on the dynamics of gathered faith communities.

You may have noticed that the subtitle for this volume is *God's Abiding Words for an Active Faith*. The textual divisions do not follow strict scholarly habit. That is, your Bible or commentary might group the subsections of these tiny letters differently than I do in this book. Instead, each session focuses on a word or theme that sheds light on teachings that the writers of these texts considered important for navigating tricky church waters. One larger texture to the words of the Johannine letters is that of God's "abiding" nature—a God who is active in our lives up close; a God who does not watch from afar, but who instead lives with us and in us!

As you use these sessions, do not become slaves to the featured "words" you find in the titles. Instead, let them inform you. Then free yourself to encounter the text personally and as a group. These "abiding words" are simply suggestions for what you may find to be a supporting notion in the text. They direct you to the prescription that the writers felt would help the church and its members. But other riches await you as you explore any of John's or Jude's teachings. Many times, no one word could summarize everything that these early church leaders entrusted to us.

What is an "active" faith? For starters, an active faith is not satisfied at the moment of acceptance. Many Christians believe that they "deal" with their faith in a onetime decision. Believing that they have been saved at a moment in their lives, they attempt to set God aside in some ways. They prefer to mark a life task off their list and get on with living. An active faith understands instead that the "decision" moment is only the beginning of the journey. As with these abiding words of John and Jude, there are teachings and stories that will attach themselves to the open spirit. They will become parts of our beliefs and our living. They will inspire, protect, inform, and challenge our faith lives such that we are not left the same. They drive us to active belief as Christ modeled. The active faith also understands key New Testament notions like "love," "faith," or "redemption" as ongoing propositions. We do not love once, nor do we love in philosophy. We love with our living for the rest of our lives. We are redeemed or renewed as we go forward in living as Christ lived. We do not love in emotion or decision only; we love biblically by our actions.

At the time I talked with Smyth & Helwys about writing for this series, a number of New Testament books were available as options. I chose these brief letters. I am fascinated with the connections of the Johannine letters to the Gospel according to John. I wanted to shed light on their continuity. I hoped to feature their application of beliefs and convictions. Likewise, Jude brought doctrine and a sense of fidelity to tradition. Among the contributions of Jude, then, is uniformity that allows believers to share in a timeless bond. We should not feel constricted by such a quality. Instead, we might sense more than ever that we are a part of something dating back to the time of Christ. We live in an age in which a word like "indoctrination" is predominantly used with negative meaning. I hope your experience of these small letters will stir your love for the church anew. They hold the potential to evoke a new appreciation for fidelity and richness of tradition. I pray they will cause you to rekindle your active dedication to the gathered body of Christ— all under the watchful eye of an abiding God!

Introducing 1, 2, 3 John and Jude

The Letters of 1, 2, 3 John in Time and Place

The letters known as 1, 2, and 3 John hold an important place in the New Testament. Yet most readers and preachers frequently pass over them completely. The letters are small and not particularly well known. Your study promises to bring back to you the familiar gems they contain, along with an introduction to some of the hidden treasures that may strengthen your faith. The specific issues to which the original writers responded, and the precise audience they addressed, remain unclear. But if the student is not put off by that uncertainty, the letters' strength will be evident. To add to our mystery, scholars differ as to who they believe wrote these letters. Furthermore, do these small writings really qualify as "letters" in the technical sense? Many agree that the normal form and content of a true letter is not found in these at all.

An image of the aging disciple named John, survivor of survivors, lends sentiment to the voicing of early Christian theology. The author "John" passes on a love-based ethic aimed at untold generations of believers to come. Indeed, John rests on his survival as a testimony that the way of truth and love is valid sustenance. The language and style of communication are simple. By one count, there are only 303 different Greek words used in 1 John, for instance.

As early as the third century, Dionysius (bishop of Alexandria) noted strong ties between the Gospel of John and these letters. Judging from language, style, and theology, there seemed to be some commonality. However, he did not feel that the Revelation of John could be traced to the same pen. John Wesley generally shared this view as well. Some modern scholars argue that even the differences between John's Gospel and these letters make their ties to a common author weak at best. A strong theory is that a Johannine "school" of followers perpetuated the teachings and theology laid out by John. Perhaps their direct experience with him gave them a shared belief, language, and style to utilize in penning these words. For the purposes of this book, we will refer to the author(s) as "John" and to the writings as "letters."

If the question of authorship is not ours to answer, what can we observe? These letters are pastoral in nature. This is a starting place for the reader. The writers care deeply about the movement of Christ, but they also care intimately for those they know in the churches. They desire peace, health, and sound belief in these churches. We can also observe that these letters stem from some situation in a particular congregation, perhaps, but seem intended for wider reading. The writings might diagnose and prescribe based on one group's dynamic, but the application yields help to believers across time and geography as they too gather in Christ's name. One issue we can observe appears to be the emerging tide of early believers who wished to affirm Jesus Christ, but who would not commit to his coming in the flesh. Certainly there was already developing rivalry and confusion about which of the emerging leaders in the church to follow. As you read, you will find other issues that are typical of group dynamics.

The language of these letters is simple in form and not burdened with style details such as those typically found in epistles of the age. Thus the difficulties with authorship and specific audiences, or issues addressed, arise. Outlining the three letters is also difficult, yet many have attempted to do so. Themes and thoughts overlap or "interweave," as some have suggested. Much as they do in the Fourth Gospel, thoughts seem to build on previous thoughts in these letters. The letters contain many reminders about things the believers "know" or "have heard." Syntax is used similarly in the Gospel and the letters. Theological development seems consistent between the writings as well. Some scholars make the observation that there is a cyclical reality to the thematic ebb and flow.

These letters appear to date to the earliest years of the second century AD. It is believed that the Gospel of John was written between AD 90–100, and the letters followed sometime later. Although tradition had the apostle John writing all of them, by the third century Origen wrote that some church leaders doubted that the same apostle wrote all the books. Eusebius believed the Gospel and 1 John were authentic, but he skeptically referred to the "so-called" Second and Third Epistles of John (McDowell, 189–90). Later Jerome, who translated the Latin Bible, said that the author of 1 John was not the same elder as the author of 2 and 3 John. Scholars do believe that all were written over a fairly brief period. Many believe these letters were written in Ephesus, the traditional location of the Johannine school of followers.

The message of the letters takes shape around a vague set of church leadership and belief issues. One can deduce that a group or groups have split off and emerged as rivals. Perhaps they were at one time members of a church that John helped start. They are now teaching and preaching, but their message differs primarily on confession of Christ as Son of God in the flesh.

Edward A. McDowell contends that the Gospel portrayal of John as one of the "Sons of Thunder" comes through in these writings (McDowell, 192). In referring to the rival leaders of his day as "false teachers," "liars," "false prophets," and even "the antichrist," John makes strong accusations. These are thought to be early leaders of what would become the Gnostics of the second century. They believed the physical body, all matter even, was so evil that it could not be of God. Therefore, they stretched views of Christ's lordship to fit their own beliefs. This included a notion that Christ might have inhabited a man at crucifixion, but that God would not have taken on flesh and walked among us. Another group believed human suffering could not be applied to deity and therefore rejected earthly images of the Christ as we would know him. Instead, these pre-Gnostics taught that people could obtain salvation through "gnosis" or knowledge. As one gained a higher realm of knowledge, one could become a more "elite" spirit. This divisive pattern of thought pitted these elite against those who simply "believed" as John and others taught. Then, as now, each movement in the early church gained followers. From John's view, the division threatened not only to splinter the fellowship but also to mislead those who came in contact with the false teachings.

The Letter by Jude

Many New Testament readers largely ignore the small letter placed just before the Revelation of John. Jude's letter consists of only twenty-five verses. The style of its writing seems apocalyptic, and its audience is unclear. Most would recognize a select few phrases of Jude without realizing their precise biblical source. Indeed, these words of doxology are commonly offered as a benediction in worship services:

> Now unto him who is able to keep you from falling, and to present you faultless before the presence of his glory with exceeding joy, to the only wise God our Savior, be glory and majesty, dominion and power, both now and forever. Amen. (Jude 24-25)

To read Jude meaningfully, the Bible student must first understand somewhat the situations that likely prompted its writing. The letter called "Jude" is actually a substitute or change of mind from what was likely intended as a treatise on a shared or common grace. Salvation was to have been the unifying thread, but the writer decided that the urgency of the moment demanded something different. Instead, an attempt to enlist believers in the battle for truth and fidelity within the early church became the chosen mode. Some have detected a finality to Jude's appeal, espousing that victory to the faithful will emerge from this rough tumble.

Authorship of Jude

"Jude" identifies himself as the brother of "James." If Jude is a short name for "Judas," then there are two candidates other than Judas Iscariot. Jude certainly seems to have been known to the writer of 2 Peter, who offers evidence of this short letter. In Luke and Acts, a son of James is referred to as Judas. There is also a brother of James, and of Jesus himself, named Judas. Most assume that this Judas is the author of this letter, but there is no certainty at this time. According to Summers, the name "Judas" was shortened for rather obvious reasons in the Christian faith. Why Jude would refer to his "brother" as James, rather than directly to the Christ, is mysterious. This writer displays a formal acquaintance with the Greek language rather than a common street-learned version. He refers back to a tradition that has been passed forward, leaning on "the apostles of our Lord Jesus Christ."

In fact, one characteristic of this writer is his staunch belief in the Christianity passed forward from the Christ by the apostles. In today's culture, such a position might get one labeled as "old school." Although only a brief amount of time had passed since the time of Christ, already the church was seeing the gospel and its theology morphing in several directions. Pre-gnostic influences are the easier problems to identify. These New Testament epistles frequently target the Gnostic counter-belief. In other cases, local church politics distorted some practices. Jude's message was valued in great part because of the identifiable fidelity to Christ's ways. The ties between this letter and 2 Peter appear strong. One might take a moment to read both in order to illuminate the study of Jude.

Jude's letter brings the reader a brief but definite application that what we believe affects how we live. Some of us come up short in living our faith, in spite of our best efforts. Others, though, view faith in Christ as a moment in time. Jude reminds us that faith is not supposed to be partitioned off to exist only on a day of the week or in a certain building. As Ray Summers says, Jude spoke to "the problem of determining the dividing line between doctrine true and false, and life true and life false" (235). Nor is faith merely a matter pertaining to eternal salvation of the soul. Life in the Christian faith is instead a journey of decision and action, of belief and test. Jude warns about various real-life heresies and makes a case for loyalty to the Christian belief.

Faithfulness: Staying Close to God

Have you ever received a letter in which other factors overshadowed the words and direct message? Perhaps seeing the sender's name on an envelope or in your e-mail inbox quickened your pulse! Maybe that letter came from someone you didn't expect to hear from. Or perhaps they wrote with an enthusiasm or love that you had not anticipated. Maybe the simple time and attention required of writing outstripped anything specific in the letter. In the end, the power of that letter rested only in part with its words. The letter of Jude is such a letter; its strength and certainty in its words of doctrine perhaps outweigh its more literal components.

The brief salutation of Jude is in proportion to the brevity of the letter. In that short greeting, however, Jude gives what few identifying clues the reader will get. He is noticeably humble about his true identity or affiliation with Christ and the apostles. His intended audience is not clarified; they only receive a kind of spiritual affiliation as "the called." This designation seems to indicate that Jude is concerned with those who have truly heard the voice of God in Christ and who have lived faithfully to that Lordship. The descriptive words "beloved" and "kept" testify to Jude's belief in the ability of God to abide victoriously with the faithful.

An Urgent Cause

In verse 3, Jude states that he intended to write on a shared or common "salvation." He was even "eager" to do so. Some speculate that the mixture of Jewish Christians with Gentile Christians was enough of an issue that he instead began to address that. Surely, division among those referred to as the Judaizers was a major threat to the early church. However, the times compelled him to write about something even more pressing. The writer of Jude was interrupted or distracted by a need to warn his readers about spiritual and institutional dangers. Their need to "contend" for their faith is a strong statement! That Greek word, in fact, suggests a military or hand-to-hand wrestling with an opponent (Summers, 236).

Jude points out something that Christians would do well to notice, that these inside threats "secretly gained admission." One can only speculate as to how much respect his warning might get today because, distracted by the impulse to respect the freedom of all believers, many would not feel any urgency about orthodoxy in the faith. Today's notion that all truth is personal and valid poses perhaps an even more urgent danger. Nonetheless, Jude asserts that some among the believers behave in ways that render them "ungodly." He says they threaten to "pervert" God's grace into false beliefs that permit "licentiousness" or lawless immorality. Jude sees them as essentially lost causes. He focuses less on redeeming these people than on how the church must turn against the effects of these ungodly individuals. This is a disturbing flavor of Jude's writing for more grace-minded readers. However, his focus demonstrates fidelity to Christ's presence and to the Bride of Christ—the church itself. To those who threaten the church, Jude deals out a measure of righteous indignation flavored with God's judgment.

Jude's warnings continue. Israel's history of deliverance out of Egypt includes a reality of destruction for those who opposed and oppressed God's chosen. Jude alludes to a celestial court that has convened around attendants who have turned from their position near the Almighty. To add emphasis, he reminds readers of the colossal destruction at the cities of Sodom and Gomorrah against those who stood opposite Jehovah.

Those Who Would Divide

Moving forward to his own day, Jude turns the attention of verse 8 back toward those who mislead and divide. In verses 8-13, it seems that these guilty live a dreamlike life. However, they only succeed in "defiling the flesh, rejecting authority, and reviling the glorious ones." Jude then invokes well-known Old Testament figures such as Cain, Moses, and Michael the Archangel to get his readers' attention. These New Testament troublemakers who draw Jude's ire do not win long-term favor with God. Instead, they blemish the festival gatherings. They are empty non-producers, reminding us of Christ's warnings about unproductive fruit trees and lazy servants.

In verse 14, Jude brings a dose of divine judgment on these who have departed the faith. What it would be like to do church with these characters? Their interruptions, stirring of opposition in church business, distraction, and challenging of teachers or preachers certainly would damage the community after a time. While differing and speaking might be within their rights, the ill effects of their activity on the Body of Christ would become evident. Perhaps you've lived this if you've been a part of a church for any time.

Among the charges, Jude characterizes these as having "abandoned themselves" in search of the pleasures and treasures that now have their attention. Like small children (and like ourselves, at times!), they are drawn to shiny, entertaining things. By verse 14, the writer quotes Enoch's prophecy, which foretells the Lord's judgment and conviction of these who have caused such trouble among God's elect. The list of characteristics in verse 16 paints a particularly incriminating picture. Jude's impatient description includes "grumblers, malcontents" and people who "follow their own passions, loud-mouthed boasters." Then there is the manipulative practice of "flattering people to gain advantage."

What can we do with these lists of offenses? What possible good can a study of Jude's indictments against New Testament troublemakers yield for twenty-first-century learners? The key may come from the sum of bothersome details the writer paints in this text. When we add them all up, one of his key values as a leader tutored by the apostles is faithfulness. Faithfulness, the opposite of many of these charges, yields practical and timeless implications. First, the Christian faith asks for our loyalty in the face of distraction and allure. Then, as now, we could claim to be part of many teams. Christ's salvation means we have chosen to stand with one side. For those who have chosen the Lordship that God offers, our days of being wishy-washy have run their course. To those who must stand up to troublemakers in their church, Jude's call is to stay close to God. This means they need to know not only that they believe in God, but also *what* they believe about God. Third, faithfulness means that being spiritually healthy requires that we remain an active part of the gathered body of Christ. The biblical narrative is not the story of "God and me." At least the truth of Christ does not end there for the believer. Rather, God's goodness for humanity is lived out in the context of a gathered people.

Jude's letter carries power. His conviction is evident and inspires us to seek similar passion about our faith and about God's church.

The writer's value for the kingdom led by Christ points us toward wanting to know more about what inspired his fervor. In a world that is often bored and difficult to impress, the author of Jude comes to us from the past, speaking of a relationship with God that is fueled by devotion and hope! The true journey with God today brings all the excitement we are able to handle.

1. Would you characterize your Christian faith more as (a) a moment in time or (b) the beginning of a journey in newness? Why? What difference does this make?

_____

_____

_____

_____

_____

2. When you think of threats to the Christian faith, what might people living during the time of Jude's letter have faced?

_____

_____

_____

_____

_____

3. Today, what barriers to our faith do we face? List as many as you can, brainstorming first and evaluating later.

_____

_____

_____

_____

4. Jude changed from his original intent to write about salvation. Instead, his letter turned into a plea for orthodoxy and loyalty. If you were writing to another group of believers today, what would seem urgent for you to write about? Why?

_____

_____

_____

_____

5. For you, what are some of the alluring "things" of this world? Asked another way, what are two or three things that seem to beckon you away from God?

_____

_____

_____

_____

6. What are some of the positive accusations that someone could make about your practice of Christian faith? What are one or two negative allegations someone could level about your practice of faith?

_____

_____

_____

_____

7. When you hear a call to "loyalty" to true Christian faith, what real-life action or value might that involve?

_____

_____

_____

_____

8. How would you summarize Jude's message so far? What is his agenda? What is the "call" of Jude's words?

_____

_____

_____

_____

Building: God's Faithful Help in Strengthening One Another

As associate pastor for pastoral care, I lead many support groups that help people cope in the aftermath of tragedy or misfortune. Life brings pain, disappointment, disillusionment, and unforeseen grief. One such group I have facilitated for more than fifteen years is Divorce Recovery. Though I have never been divorced, I have noticed a few things about divorcees in general. One is that in spite of their tremendous hurt, they coalesce quickly around the commonality of their shared experience. Once put in a group of fellow divorcees, most draw deeply from the knowledge that they are not so alone after all. Relationships seem to form more quickly among fellow divorcees than in almost any other support cohort.

Nobody likes to hear the words, "I told you so!" But in this case, there may be some perverse comfort for the embattled audience of Jude to hear that the apostles had warned them. As in a support group, the comfort comes from being in the company of others who know the extent and source of their troubles. The apostles had warned them that some would oppose their fledgling movement of Christianity. Apparently, the apostles' warning fits the bill for what is happening in the early church this letter is written to. Believers surrounded by those who don't believe!

Ray Summers approaches his commentary on Jude with the assumption that a primary reason for the letter was to counter "scoffers," individuals or groups who caused trouble in the church by ridiculing or opposing with cynicism. What were these people doing that was so bad? Shouldn't everyone be free to speak his or her conscience and have a voice in God's church? In 2 Peter, the "scoffers" cast doubt on the belief in the second coming of Christ. Specifically, Summers deduces that the scoffers in Jude set up divisions within the fellowship (238–39). The scoffers are described as "worldly" and following "un-godly passions."

Earl Johnson says these scoffers are persons who do not "have the gifts of the Holy Spirit." Further, they "make fun" of the believers who have the gifts and presence of God in their lives. Verses 22-23 note some of the specific characteristics of these scoffers. Here, the writer of Jude identifies "doubters," those "who are already in the fire" and some who are "contaminated by the ungodly" (Johnson, 150–51).

How does one speak to such a serious issue in the fellowship? The writer of Jude employs pastoral encouragement to the loyal in order to strengthen them. We cannot compel others to believe what they are not ready to accept. Likewise, there are limits to which aspects of our friends' and neighbors' behaviors we can influence. However, in much of life, certain countering or shaping actions are within our bounds. In brief, the writer of Jude will coach his listeners toward behaviors that might help the situation—and that of today's Christians too.

Build Yourselves Up

Charles Erdman, in his commentary on the "general" epistles, sees this section of Jude as pivotal: "Here at last, the epistle reaches its climax. Not in the description of the false teachers and their doom; but in their exhortation, addressed to the faithful followers of Christ, the real purpose of Jude is fulfilled" (Erdman, 183).

First, Jude encourages Christians to work at strengthening their knowledge and experience of what they believe: "But you, beloved, build yourselves up on your most holy faith; pray in the Holy Spirit; keep yourselves in the love of God; wait for the mercy of our Lord Jesus Christ unto eternal life." What can we do to gain spiritual strength?

First, advises Jude, we keep ourselves "in the love of God." Or, as Summers writes, "Let God's love be the area of their entire thought and life" (239). This echoes much of Paul's writing, where we are encouraged to focus on things that are holy, uplifting, and good. Lest this sound too limiting or Pollyanna-like, there is a sound acknowledgment that we are ultimately products of that to which we give our time and energy.

Second, we should "wait for the mercy of our Lord Jesus Christ unto eternal life." That is, the faithful should have a longer glance than the short-term vision of the scoffer. Those who divide or make fun might limit their focus to the issue or belief at hand. For Christians, the prize always lies ahead in the eternal nature of salvation in Christ. Granted, there will be trying moments and painful times when it will be difficult to wait for the ultimate justice or security of eternal life. However, the perspective is there all the same.

Finally, Jude couches all of our spiritual activity in prayer. The believer stays connected with God, involved in open and ongoing conversation. The scoffer is in touch with himself and his friends. Prayer is the easily overlooked constant.

Be Versatile in Outreach and Service

The profession of ministry, or clergy, has been termed "The Last Bastion of Generalization in an Age of Specialization" (Hollingsworth, 2004). One challenge of being the people of Christ is to reckon clearly with who we are and who we are not. While most resist the more limiting frames of thought, if we are honest, we agree that each church has a personality. So does each believer, of course. We have unique spiritual profiles. Try as they may, neither churches nor believers can be all things for all people.

However, we have a variety of gifts, ideas, and techniques at our disposal. To the extent that we can develop our personhood, versatility will serve us well. The writer of Jude provides a quick overview of some of the ways that the church can redeem or sway those who resist. The lesson might not be limited to these issues, either. Instead, the list could prompt us to explore further the kind of work God wants us to do in our relationships.

For instance, we are reminded that we should try to "convince some who doubt" (v. 22). While apologetics may not always save the day, we occasionally have a chance to reason with some who doubt. C. S. Lewis's story includes mention of a motorcycle ride he took with his brother. The two of them headed to visit a zoo. As the story goes, Lewis rode in the sidecar while his brother drove. When the trip began, Lewis did not believe in God through Christ. After conversing during the ride, they arrived at the zoo, and Lewis believed! (Lewis Institute). The writer of Jude also suggests that we should "save some by redeeming them" (v. 22). While humans can reach a point of loss beyond which they will not turn back, it is ultimately between them and God to decide if they will be redeemed. The unbeliever might be involved in an unfolding drama of redemption at the next turn of the day. The grace of Christ is one gift we have to offer to those in need. That act of inclusion and acceptance may be the story that, otherwise, we do not have words to tell. Verse 23 instructs, "On some, have mercy with fear." That is, we have mercy without becoming that on which we have mercy. Said another way, we can love within boundaries, lest we get too close to the same fires that would also burn us. As a counselor friend of mine is fond of saying, "love and sympathize, but don't own their issues!"

The Benediction

Verses 24-25 may be the most recognizable words found in Jude. They have graced worship services across the world. This benediction, or doxology, serves as a fitting close to a worship service. The words comfort and energize all at the same time.

When heard in their context, verses 24-25 speak to a people threatened by confusing forces at work among them. The writer's words affirm a God who is "able" in answer to the scoffers' divisive guffawing. And God is not just generally able, but specifically strong enough to prevent our "falling." Presumably, we might fall into disbelief or "false" belief. At the least, the threat of falling in the charge of heresy loomed at that time as well. Then, there is the notion that we can make our way successfully along the journey heavenward into the presence of God "without blemish." This suggests a supernatural transformation, for none of us could harbor such hope without the saving and redemptive power of Christ. Notice that all this *will* happen, according to Jude, and not by the narrowest of margins. Who hasn't waltzed through a test, an interview, or a meeting unprepared? The reaction is often "Whew!" rather than anything we would describe as "rejoicing" (v. 24).

The pushback against early Gnostic or false teachers continues in the closing verse. These words are offered "to the only God, our Savior through Jesus Christ our Lord, be glory, majesty, dominion, and authority, before all time and now and forever. Amen." The "only" God is an obvious reference to the many "gods" who would prevail in that (and any!) age. In fact, the Gnostic influence was later known as presenting many "demigods" (Summers, 239). One last declaration is made that this God is "our" Savior—the one we have known, Jesus Christ. He will last. He will be sufficient now and forevermore.

1. Can you remember a time when someone essentially said, "I told you so," and they were correct? Was your reaction positive or negative? Did their knowledge help you before the situation happened? If so, how?

_____
_____
_____
_____

2. Who are the challenging or cynical voices in your life? What good purpose do they serve? How can their words hurt your causes?

_____
_____
_____
_____

3. How can today's church both honor its grand tradition and employ a versatility that helps it continue to thrive (or even to live)?

_____
_____
_____
_____

4. What could a church do to become more self-aware about its unique giftedness and "personality" under God?

_____
_____
_____
_____

5. How effective is it to argue the merits of the Gospel with someone who does not believe as you do? Why? How are we to respond to "scoffers"?

_____
_____
_____
_____

6. Especially in the more hellfire-and-brimstone traditions, the notion of standing before God seems like an unnerving experience. Imagine you are standing before God. What do you feel emotionally? Spiritually? Why?

_____

_____

_____

_____

7. Do you believe God is "able"? Why or why not?

_____

_____

_____

_____

8. How do you maintain the loving, redemptive action toward others to which Christ calls you while maintaining your own boundaries and values?

_____

_____

_____

_____

Presence and Forgiveness: God with Us as a Giver of Life

1 Jn 1:1-10

The words of today's text ring oddly familiar in our ears. In fact, they sound like the words of Christmas. So closely related to the thoughts found in the Gospel of John's first chapter, the text from 1 John sounds like a slightly different translation. In fact, stop if you will and read for yourself from John's Gospel:

> In the beginning was the Word, and the Word was with God, and the Word was God. He was with God in the beginning. Through him all things were made; without him nothing was made that has been made. In him was life, and that life was the light of men. The light shines in the darkness, but the darkness has not understood it. There came a man who was sent from God; his name was John. He came as a witness to testify concerning that light, so that through him all men might believe.

When we drive through my wife's small hometown, we enjoy the dramatic contrast from the large city where we live now. Nestled in the Piedmont foothills of middle Georgia is this historic railroad town of no more than 4,000 people. The pace is noticeably slower there, and we relax as soon as we drive into the town limits. Sometimes, though, there are so few people out and about that you begin to feel isolated. At night, things change. From the top of the little mountain on which Elizabeth was raised, one can look off into that same small town. In the darkness, you would insist you were looking down on New York, Chicago, or Los Angeles. Lights are everywhere in the distance, signaling that you are far from alone. They glisten and interrupt an otherwise blanket of black. Suddenly, you feel that you are part of a community that is very much alive!

Presence

Two themes emerge quickly here from the Johannine school of thought. First, an attendant God intentionally created humanity. Christ eternal has been a part of shaping life and kingdom, overseeing all that was set in motion up to this very moment. Expressed in terms such as "truth" or "light," Christ has now dwelt among us. Among the outcomes of that presence is a gathered community of believers who share the security and hope of God. In fact, central to these writings is the sense that God is an "abiding" presence among us. This up-close presence of a God stands in stark contrast to other images that some portray. John moves away from prevailing notions of a distant, brooding, angry, or vengeful ruler.

There is a reason for all this talk of the presence of an abiding God. The writer of 1 John is trying to counter the opposing voices at work in many of the early churches, specifically those viewed as the precursors to the second-century Gnostics. Already, some argued that God would not have stooped to exist outside the heavens, especially in human form. They viewed the physical body as corrupt or defiled. A pure Almighty would never assume such a dwelling, they argued.

John's words in the opening lines of this first letter reflect his wish to substantiate a real Christ. He says,

> That which was from the beginning, which we have heard, which we have seen with our eyes, which we have looked upon and touched with our hands, concerning the word of life—the life was made manifest, and we saw it, and testify to it, and proclaim to you the eternal life which was with the Father and was made manifest to us—that which we have seen and heard we proclaim also to you . . . . (1:1-3a)

There is no mistaking John's claim to have been among those who knew Jesus Christ in a firsthand and personal way. In a day before pictures, video, or voice recordings, writers often attempted this type of descriptive credentialing. John assures his readers that the abiding God has lived and walked with creation.

The word rendered "beginning" in many translations reflects the eternal nature of Christ with God. The writer uses a Greek word consistent with that used in John 1:1 to speak of a "beginning" which included a *creation with Christ*. The stipulation that authority comes from one "which we have heard" evokes the Gospel of

John's notion that Jesus was the "Word," or *logos* in the Greek. This seems to refer to the Christ himself. The description continues as it establishes a sense of testimony by including that this "truth" is also one "which we have seen." Some will struggle with the notion that the disciple John might not have directly authored these writings. However, many scholars of the day believe that if John passed this teaching directly to his followers, then they could claim direct knowledge. Further strengthening his claim, the writer adds that this One is a person "we have touched," or *handled* in the Greek. Concerning the "word of life" again, this is the same usage as for Christ in John 1. This concept harkens back to the Old Testament Hebrew concept of *dabar*, or Word of God that is *a projection of the one who uttered it himself!*

Second, there is a sacred community that embodies this faith in Christ. These gathered believers share in the gifts and qualities left to us by Jesus. These words are written in the hopes of stabilizing the early church "so that you may have fellowship with us; and our fellowship is with the Father and with his Son Jesus Christ. And we are writing this that our joy may be complete" (1:3b-4). Faith in Christ will demand not only a belief, but a gathered life with others who practice this same faith. Lives informed by this belief will show evidence that something is different.

In verse 2, we see mention of eternal life that "was with the Father" and is now accessible to us! The reader might easily miss this, but it is a fairly loaded counter to another Gnostic flavor of faith knowledge and status that was available only to the elite who believed rightly. John establishes that this truth is available to all, and not just to the "elite" who try to run things. In verse 3 he further establishes the benefits of Christian community in saying that "we share with *all* of you this eternal life from the Father." This stands in stark contrast to an elitist mentality then and now. It also expands the intent to include God's whole creation, which at that time might still have seemed a shocking notion.

What will result from this expansion? John says this truth is shared "so that you may have fellowship or community [*koinonia*] with us"; this is specifically in contrast to the present fellowship that was occasionally interrupted by opposing forces that threatened to invade the church and distract or divide with false teaching. But there is one more layer to this notion of *koinonia*. There is an even more important invitation to the believer to share in fellowship with "with the Father, too, and with the Son."

Forgiveness

For all his talk about the inclusiveness of community, John does not describe a life that is always easy to live. Within that community of believers, and in God's company, there is the expectation of forgiveness. There is also a quality John refers to as "light." Many believers ought to test their basic theology in part because of John's reminder that "in him there is no darkness at all" (v. 5). John affirms that God is the author of goodness and love. We must go elsewhere to partition our pain and evil. God in Christ has not only come to live among us, but has set a standard of health and goodness. Therefore, our standard of behavior will be held up against the "light" that reveals us for what we are. In fact, John clarifies that to live in "darkness" while proclaiming to be "light" is impossible.

> If we say we have fellowship with him while we walk in darkness, we lie and do not live according to the truth; but if we walk in the light, as he is in the light, we have fellowship with one another, and the blood of Jesus his Son cleanses us from all sin. If we say we have no sin, we deceive ourselves, and the truth is not in us. If we confess our sins, he is faithful and just, and will forgive our sins and cleanse us from all unrighteousness. (1:6-9)

One of the barriers to our understanding of God's forgiveness is our difficulty in comprehending how it works. Many Christians have been nurtured to understand forgiveness as a wish or a good intention to be granted. Most also view the act of forgiveness as consisting of a set of words spoken at a moment in time. By extension, then, these acts of forgiveness seem either to work or to fail. But we have other issues with the notion of sin and forgiveness. In today's supposedly postmodern culture, some struggle to acknowledge the existence of "sin," as we can explain away so much of life as individual preference. Thus, a personalized sense of right and wrong could virtually eliminate the notion of sin from the theological landscape. Then, there is the issue of the human tendency toward occasional acts of hypocrisy. That is, we hold others to standards by which we ourselves are not bound to live.

John attributes to God the ability to flex with human frailty. If we are willing to confess our shortcomings, we will find our God faithful to grant the forgiveness our souls so badly need. However, John would stress that we must undertake this cleansing and renewing honestly. To say we have no sin and therefore need no forgiveness is to live apart from God, John says. Living with God and living without confession and forgiveness are mutually exclusive conditions. The two must travel together if we are to enjoy a genuine presence with God. The strong language of making God a "liar" (v. 10) expresses the certainty with which John holds the conviction. Notice that John says this contradiction—saying we fellowship with God while we walk in darkness—indicates that God's "word" is not in us. Remember that this "truth" is Jesus Christ himself, according to Johannine thought.

The Net of It All?

In today's economy, the fruits of our relative wealth have now shaped generations since World War II. With that affluence has come the expectation of a customized or individualized experience with consumer goods and services, to be sure. But many believe this individualization has brought with it an isolating effect. Now more than ever, believers need to hear John reminding us that healthy Christian fellowship is not only a source of joy but also a source of completeness.

We still must guard against false teachers, piety, and elitism within God's kingdom. We still get distracted by all manner of things that seem more pleasant, fun, or even important. We get caught up in dynamics that seek to define who is "in" and who is "out." It is difficult enough for us to accept that forgiveness is possible from God. It seems just as hard, at times, to grant forgiveness to others or to ourselves. As followers after the Truth, we must connect with the renewing and fellowshipping power of believing in the Giver of Light whom John proclaims. This is not a God who excludes or a Lord who stands at arm's length. In John's view, the abiding sense of God permeates all of life. Our God is present and up close. Christ is for *all* . . . that *our* joy might be complete.

1. What seems to be the writer's purpose for 1 John, as expressed in verses 1-5?

_____

_____

_____

_____

2. In your life, with which places or groups do you feel included? Why? When do you tend to feel alone or isolated? Why?

_____

_____

_____

_____

3. What ingredients go into making a credible witness, as you think in terms of court testimony or persuasive presentations at your workplace?

_____

_____

_____

_____

4. How do such diverse understandings of our God, and our Bible, seem to make their way into church life with Christians?

_____

_____

_____

_____

5. As you approach church and your life of faith, in honesty, would you describe yourself as more of a consumer individual or community-oriented believer? Why? What might be important about evaluating yourself on this aspect?

_____

_____

_____

_____

6. Who has been instrumental in bringing to your life the word of Truth? How so? Was this through their teaching? Through their living? Through their particular goodness?

_____

_____

_____

_____

7. When you think of forgiveness, is your concept more of a moment in time or of a process that takes time?

_____

_____

_____

_____

8. How do you know when you have forgiven someone? How do you know when someone has forgiven you?

_____

_____

_____

_____

9. What is it about God that gives you certainty of "grace" or forgiveness? What causes you to be less certain?

_____

_____

_____

_____

Identity: Knowing and Obeying the Life Call of Christ

1 Jn 2:1-6

Are you a deadline person? Do you seem to work better when your parameters are clearly set, or are you more productive when you are free? While we might instinctively wish for freedom, most of us probably need structure and definition. Likewise, a high school friend of mine told me an unlikely tale about a prom night experience. His sister was the beautiful captain of the cheerleaders. Predictably, she was dating a football team captain as prom season rolled around. That night, as she prepared to leave the house, she asked her parents for a curfew. Amazing as that might be, it gets better. Her parents responded that they trusted her. She thanked them, but said that she really wanted to know what time they expected her home. Finally, the three of them agreed upon a reasonable hour and, sure enough, she was home a few minutes before. The imposition of a curfew communicated care and love to her.

The Advocate

The writer of 1 John uses this frame of mind as chapter 2 opens. He knows that his audience may try to live within God's healthy bounds. They may truly desire to live in step with their loving Creator. But realistically, they need the guidance of confession and reconciliation from time to time. This fragile human people will inevitably step outside of God's greatest hope and commit sin. This is where the writer opens the section.

In verse 1, "Jesus Christ the righteous" is the title applied to our Lord. It is worth noting that the writer of 1 John uses the aorist tense here to communicate that he wants them not to sin in the first place. Had he used the present tense, it would suggest that they were already sinning and he wants them to stop (McDowell, 199). It is as though he knows they will sin, but still expects them to try not to sin. But as they do sin, there is an answer. The word is *paraklētos*, suggesting an "advocate." This is the same word used for "Holy Spirit" in John's Gospel to convey "one called alongside to help, counsel or represent." McDowell says that Jesus as Advocate is *pros con patera* or "with the father," suggesting a close and intimate relationship.

In verse 2, how does this transact? The word *hilasmos*, translated "expiation," suggests something that covers. The idea seems not to soothe or appease God about our wrongdoing. Rather, Jesus removes or alters the cause of the alienation in the first place. He becomes the means provided by the Father for reconciling the sinner to God. In some sense, Jesus gets between us and our God, at least in the area of sin.

How Can We Know Him?

Next, the writer concerns himself with the idea of obedience. If the reader values confidence, here is a way to gain some. I can remember my own youth group days. We'd gather at a neighborhood home for our church's youth Bible study. Somebody would strum a guitar as we sang "We Are One in the Spirit." The song includes a line that goes "and they'll know we are Christians by our love." First John 2 gives us one way to feel in step with Christ by saying, "And by this we may be sure that we know him, if we keep his commandments" (v. 3). Why, that's great news, until the sobering moment when we realize how difficult it sometimes is to keep the commandments.

As believers, we sometimes find ourselves musing on the certainty of our faith. While we may talk about "knowing," though, most of us are not always confident. *What if there's something about truly accepting salvation through the Lordship of Christ that I've missed? How does this spiritual transaction between God the Father and Jesus the Son work, anyway?* John gives us this good news/bad news assurance. But there is one more question—*Just how does obedience equal assurance?* John appears convinced that one is not likely to obey consistently without first experiencing Christ in a way that drives such values. Thus his thought in verse 3 about our being sure: *if* we keep the commandments, *then* we "may be sure that we know him." The verb *ginōskō*, from which the label of Gnostic emerged later, speaks to a sure knowledge or close experience. Just as our obedience is evidence of our closeness with Christ, our closeness with Christ is what drives us to want to live as free of sin as possible

(v. 4). That is, our closeness influences us to live in obedience to the Master.

Our Words Proven

Bill Curry is the football coach of the Georgia State University Panthers. He played under the legendary Vince Lombardi with the Green Bay Packers and later as a teammate of Johnny Unitas with the Baltimore Colts. During his Colts years, Curry says the team always let Unitas have the last word in the locker room before taking the field. As the team's hype reached a fever pitch, various players would yell about what they were going to do to the opponent that day. Then, inevitably, their gaze fell on Unitas. Propped in the doorway, the future hall-of-famer glared at his team and often said, "Talk is cheap, boys!" Reminded, they sprinted out to back up their claims on the field.

John follows his own line of thought by creating a proof. He knows that talk is cheap. John's verse 4 movement is to remind the audience that we can fool ourselves and others sometimes, but our actions will prove whether the truth is within us.

Likewise, those who consistently live by Christ's truth and love will bear evidence of that. When we do so, we "keep his word." John now uses the word *agapē* for "love." As many know, this word connotes "the love of God" or a love uniquely lived out in the way God loves. God's love abides in us if we keep his word and live obediently. In "perfecting" this love of God, the notion is that this love is brought to fruition or fulfillment. We can only express this godly love in one way—living as Christ (McDowell, 200). Today, as then, our churches are often actively "run" by those who talk the best game, so to speak. Churches frequently embody the message of the popular bumper sticker, "The world is run by those who bother to show up!" Too often we are led by those who are first to speak up, or who impress others as being, well, impressive. In God's inverted kingdom, the subtler voices of wisdom may come from the edges of the room and speak up less often. Perhaps we need more disciplined ways of discerning who really has shown up.

What's at Stake?

There is an obvious tension for the astute reader of this text. On the one hand, Paul's words play in our heads from Romans 3:23: "All have sinned and fallen short of the glory of God." We are plagued by this reality. We wonder if we can be redeemed, and in our worst moments we may at least muse on how something as definite as assurance is even possible.

In adult Christian education, it is assumed that one of the burning questions learners bring to church each week is "So what?" We should not miss the importance of the brand of confidence John advocates. It's not contrived or wishful confidence. It's not the misplaced confidence in things that matter little. Instead, John speaks of confidence where it matters. Our souls are steadied and quieted when we are able to perceive the nearness of God. We are able to be what Christ wants us to be when we are sure about things that matter in eternity. If we journey with Christ, we long to be "sure" that we are in him. This might be true whether your focus is on salvation or on living a life that actually matters here on earth. Either way, with Christ as our guide, John says we can have confidence.

It should matter also that love is perfected. Christ's life and teachings were modeled in acts of love. Paul especially took up that cause in his writings, systematizing a theology built on love. Let us be clear about this love that John espouses: New Testament love is more about action than feeling. Love is more about living than liking. We are incapable of accepting or liking everybody we meet. However, we are called to "love" them all. We often must resolve to live out Christ's love regardless of what we feel. This is not a false or fake way of living. Rather, choosing to love as Christ loved is a strong resolve that often demands power from above. John states that as we keep God's word, in us God's love is truly perfected. Which of us deeply, honestly wants to stand in the way of God's perfecting love?

1. Who are the adults in your life that you grant relational "permission" to address you as "my little child"? What qualities might earn them this intimate place in your life?

_____
_____
_____
_____

2. Today's supposedly post-modern culture does not seem to believe much in "sin." Why is this? How would you explain "sin" to a person today?

_____

_____

_____

_____

3. If you were to write a concise, one-sentence definition of "sin," what would you say?

_____

_____

_____

_____

4. Going beyond reciting the Ten Commandments from the Old Testament, what does "keeping God's commands" mean to you?

_____

_____

_____

_____

5. If each of us has sinned and fallen short (Rom 3:23) of God's will, then what is the truth in verse 4 for our lives?

_____

_____

_____

_____

6. As less than perfect humans, how can any of us find assurance that we know Christ truly? Discuss this in your group and see what hope you can offer each other.

_____

_____

_____

_____

Identity: Knowing and Obeying the Life Call of Christ

7. How can we understand a New Testament concept of "love" that does not require that we necessarily *like* everyone we know? Why is this crucial for growing spiritually and for loving as Christ loved?

_____

_____

_____

_____

8. What might it mean that God's love is working toward being "perfected" in us? How would you explain this to someone new to the faith or considering Christianity?

_____

_____

_____

_____

Consistency: The Old Commandment Is the New

1 Jn 2: 7-11

Peter Marshall tells the following story, which I admit leaves my head spinning.

In the days of the American Revolutionary War, there lived at Ephrata, Pennsylvania, a Baptist pastor by the name of Peter Miller, who enjoyed the friendship of General Washington. There also dwelt in that town one Michael Wittman, an evil-minded man who did everything in his power to abuse and oppose this pastor. Michael Wittman later committed treason and eventually was arrested and sentenced to death. The old preacher started out on foot and walked the whole seventy miles to Philadelphia to plead for Wittman's life. He was admitted into Washington's presence and at once begged for the life of the traitor.

Washington said, "No, Peter, I cannot grant you the life of your friend." The preacher exclaimed, "My friend? He is the bitterest enemy I have." Washington cried, "What? You've walked seventy miles to save the life of an enemy? Why?"

Miller is said to have responded, "Jesus did the same for me. I can do no less."

"Then that puts the matter in a different light," Washington apparently said. "I will grant the pardon." And he did (Marshall, 323–24).

The Old Becomes New

When is something new not really new at all? Sometimes an old truth suddenly becomes understandable or doable because of a change in our lives. This is the case for the Christian believer, as being reconciled with God is now possible through the life and salvation of Jesus. God's hope for humanity had not changed since the earliest pages of Genesis. From the beginning, God actively worked to redeem humanity.

Let's face it: if you've read much of 1 John, a good bit of it is rebuke. It's interesting that when we must deliver bad news, there's usually not a good enough way to phrase that news to avoid the recipient from saying we were cruel to them. I've noticed that in my ministry, if I have to break it to someone that I disagree with them or if I have to refuse a request, they'll usually go and tell someone I wasn't nice to them. But maybe I *was* nice to them; they just didn't like what I had to say.

First John begins this section with a name, "Beloved." As William Barclay observes, the writer of 1 John begins this section on *loving* with the very *act* of loving by referring to his audience in this way (51). If you read the Gospel of John and these short letters, you'll know that's the voice of John. The Law itself was best intended to help humans live together in healthy, fair, and loving ways. Leviticus 19:18 says, "Thou shalt love thy neighbor as thyself." John's news is "old" in that this isn't the first time his readers have heard the command. They know they are to love. So do you and I.

Our cat knows she isn't supposed to claw at the carpet on the bottom stair. This isn't a new thought. I've told her myself, and often, but she does it at least weekly. She makes a big production of stretching forward and getting just the right spot, and then I see her start to paw at the carpet or I hear the sound of her claws. I have to say, "No!" Then she stops and looks at me because she's been squirted a million times with the "no bottle" that cat experts say one should use. She acts like this is a completely new thought, me telling her "no" about scratching the carpet. Then she runs away! I get tired of the drama. I know she knows.

That's the notion behind the writer of 1 John saying that this is an old command. The hearers of these writings *know*. In fact, some would argue that Jesus sets forth teachings on the tough act of "loving" much more clearly in the Gospels than John does here in these writings. You and I know, too.

D. Moody Smith said in his commentary on 1 John that the "Christian faith has an essential historical dimension or component: its past is authoritative. At the same time, faith looks to the future—for the future belongs to God" (62). We've been told in the past to love one another. We've been instructed to take on the pain of others who are suffering even if it isn't always our business. We've been called upon to notice the one who can do no better and needs the compassion of one who can do better, at least in that moment. We are even told to tolerate that which is intolerable until some good can be advanced, or to include those we don't readily include because God's kingdom includes them, and to forgive those who shouldn't be forgiven because God might already have forgiven them!

The Stubborn Love of God

An important characteristic makes an old notion new: God's love has determination. People outside our faith might think God is a God of fierce judgment. But when we accept Christ's salvation, we do so because we've found that God actually loves far more fiercely, or more determinedly, than God judges. God has loved us stubbornly. In the end, that determination took a winding road and delivered the Christ Babe to humanity's doorstep and ultimately on to the cross and the tomb of Easter.

The old commandment was to love your neighbor as yourself. The new command is to love as Christ has loved. In that command, the notion is taken to a higher standard! Here is a caution: if I am to love you as I love myself, some days you might not get loved so well. If I am to love you as Christ first loved you, that kind of love might be of good to you. Christ's kind of love might stand the fickle whims of my attention span, might weather the pain and disappointment life has visited upon me, and might still do you good.

Here is something else you might be able to take with you from this study. When we become Christians, we try to work up a sentimental, emotional love to get along with each other. Many of us think we're supposed to like everybody, which I gave up on a long time ago. We find instead that it's a matter of the will and not always of the emotions. You must make up your mind that you will allow God's love to reach others through you. You don't act as if you love them, but you sometimes have to determine to love them as God is determined to love you. God's love is stubborn, not always warm and fuzzy like we try to make it.

John says, "God is love" (1 John 4:8). Christ was delivered for our sins through the determined will of God. When Christ came, he was determined to love sinners. There was never a sinner Christ hated. His judgment against sin was always undercut with a loving call. Publicans and sinners were drawn to him, and even the lowest wept at his feet. The greatest thing about Christ's love was the way it touched the lives of his enemies. Jesus said, "Greater love hath no man than this, that a man lay down his life for his friends" (John 15:13). However, Jesus laid down his life for his enemies. Of course, he was his enemies' best friend, but they didn't realize it until it was too late. Love goes beyond sentimental emotions and is willed as we determine to love the person—sometimes in spite of the person.

In verse 8, John suggests that we must live a life of Christian love so the darkness will pass away. That is, in verses 9-11, our practice of love is part of God's abiding plan for interrupting the darkness of humanity. Those who walk in the light practice love; those who walk in darkness practice hatred. These are indicators of what is happening inside our spirits under the watchful eye of a loving God. The birth of Christ was the dawning of a new day for all humanity. He spread the Light of light before them as he ministered in a world of darkness. We read in Matthew's Gospel, "The people who sat in darkness saw a great light; and to them which sat in the region and shadow of death light is sprung up" (4:16 KJV).

Many scholars point out that in the Hebrew language of the Old Testament, the word for "compassion" comes from the root word for "womb." The picture is of a birthing. Something new is being born. If we apply this in human experience, it means our compassionate acts, our will to love, always give the other person another chance. I do not hold past failures against him or her. I offer a "fresh start." This is a struggle for many of us, but I want this for myself from others. Am I willing to give it to the other person?

Actively Loving One Another

To suggest that we are simply to "love" seems like a trite ending. This Scripture is much too earthy and grounded for that. Notice, then, something very real: such compassion will dramatically change the way we relate to each other. John reminds his readers of God's love extended to them through forgiveness. Because of God's compassion, our new birth is possible. Now that same compassion gives others a fresh start as we extend it to them. Our love for one another creates the world's thirst for God. Our creation of pain for each other causes the world to turn away from our Christian faith.

At another time, Jesus said, "A new command I give you: Love one another. As I have loved you, so you must love one another. By this, all will know that you are my disciples if you love one another" (John 13:34-35 NIV). Jesus spoke these words at the last Passover meal. He had just demonstrated love's willingness to serve by washing their feet.

In the divorce recovery groups I lead, we have a tough session on "forgiveness." I believe the church has done people a disservice by teaching the guilt-producing command to "forgive" without also teaching that this involves more than a feeling or a word. We've made this real life transaction sound like it can be done as easily as flipping a switch to turn off a light. In reality, true forgiveness can take years to accomplish if the hurt was deep enough. In the same way, "loving" one another may sometimes be a messy business. I think it's time we were honest about that.

So the old commandment really is the new. What's at stake in all this? Why does it matter whether we get this right? Here's a troubling thought at the end: "He does not know where he is going [the writer says of the one who "hates"], because the darkness has blinded him." The principle is that sometimes we can lose our healthy focus when we major on things that are less than what God wants us to notice.

Or, as one scholar has noticed, the English translations sometimes make verse 10 unclear as to who might stumble. We probably read this and infer that we are not to cause others to stumble. The Greek seems to leave open the possibility that *we* stumble if we do not love our brother or sister (Barclay, 57). That is, love is the one thing that enables us to make progress in life, and hatred is the one thing that makes progress impossible.

Preaching classes often ask students to grade their peers as they preach. On one such occasion, a student marked on a form "nice sermon . . . but I don't know what you want me to *do* as a result of hearing this." As with any sermon, we must ultimately decide for ourselves what we will do with John's words. Another interesting character of our day, Dr. Phil McGraw, is fond of saying that the number one "relational" rule of life is, "You either get it or you don't!"

Oddly, God might view this one the same way. Living out the old commandment in a new way involves mystery and trust, but God gave us the Gospels of Christ to show us living models. The letters of the New Testament spell out practical applications further. At least we have those helps. I admit I'm trying to live by this one while I'm also still trying to get it. If we're honest with one another, that's part of the Christian journey.

1. What is the most surprising gesture of friendship you've experienced? How did this affect your relationship with that person?

_____

_____

_____

_____

2. What is the most extreme action you've ever undertaken in the name of friendship?

_____

_____

_____

_____

3. Have you ever had to break bad news to someone, or even simply tell them "no," and they felt you had mistreated them? Were you able to clarify the intent of the situation? How?

_____

_____

_____

_____

4. Many Christians report that even the most familiar Biblical texts take on new meaning as they grow in faith and life experience. Is there a Bible passage that has taken on a completely different meaning as you've grown and changed?

_____

_____

_____

_____

5. Is there a pattern in your life that doesn't bring the best results but is difficult for you to change? Other than knowing you need to do something differently, what might help?

_____

_____

_____

_____

6. What might be the difference between "loving" someone and "liking" them? Which of these is Christ's call the clearest about?

_____

_____

_____

_____

7. Describe what you believe "forgiveness" really is. What truths should the church teach about forgiveness?

_____

_____

_____

_____

8. In what ways could our acts of compassion give a new "birth" to others in our lives?

_____

_____

_____

_____

6 Tension: Do Not Love the World?

Talk about tension! This teaching of John creates tension between two basic realities of life. On the one hand, we are to love all others. This much is clear, and Jesus and Paul are both specific about a brand of love that includes even our enemies. On the other hand, we also encounter teachings like the one in this text from 1 John. They warn us against "loving" something referred to as the "world." How can we reconcile two seemingly conflicting notions? Or, even if you are past the idea that they conflict, have you figured out how this actually translates to our daily living? There is much work to be done with this text.

Especially in more pious Christian circles, we hear talk about "the world." The rather charismatic streak that went through my home church youth group involved a lot of God talk for a while. Chief among the approved lingo was the term "worldly." As in, "Oh, she's really worldly," to reflect judgment of a poor soul who was "living in sin." It took me a while to realize that we are all living in sin! Or someone might refer to "worldly" pursuits to reflect a division between our spiritual lives and the rest of life.

The writer begins by demonstrating spiritual benefits of living life with Christ. By knowing the character of Christ and by growing in our knowledge of our faith, we enjoy positive outcomes. John affirms these outcomes as he opens the section. He addresses his thoughts to three audience designations: "children," "fathers," and "young men." For those who are put off by most biblical translations when the language is left true to the "male" address, I will not adequately solve the issue for you. Let us acknowledge the day and times of our Bible's writings; certainly in teachings such as this, the writers did not intend to leave out the female segment of believers from these truths. My hope is that you will push through any frustrations the language may cause and hear the heart of the message instead.

Who Is the Audience Again?

If the message is not limited to children, fathers, and young men, then what are we all to hear? It would seem that John spoke to three distinct stages of spiritual development more than to any gender or age group. A favorite designation for his audience was "children" or "little children." To this group, he offered basic or understandable truths. There are different possibilities for discerning what John intended. One view is to assume that John referred these writings to the whole congregation and used these terms to remind them of the different roles they occupied in each other's lives. Rather than point to specific persons, these titles might illustrate the various qualities generally present in any congregation.

In contrast, one writer has suggested that these three groups might represent three corresponding offices or levels of service within the early church; namely, that these might be comparable to deacons, elders, or bishops (Barker, 319–20). For instance, the use of "fathers" might have followed a more Jewish view that senior members of a congregation were regarded as one would regard a father in a family unit. This speaks to experience and a legacy of commitment or accomplishment.

Whether precise or not, this phrase reminds us that not all believers in our churches have reached the same degree of Christian maturity. Like literal children, we all must move from the moment of acceptance through stages of Christian development. As we learn and experience, we hope to move toward greater God-given wisdom. John's goal, then, was to address the entire congregation.

To the "children," John offers assurance. Their sins are forgiven (1 Jn 2:12) because they "know" the Father. They can enjoy fellowship with the Father. We can access God's presence through the Spirit. Access and salvation are two basic reassurances important to those who are beginning their journey of faith. This is not merely emotional cheerleading on John's part. He did not offer these words for a feel-good effect. He met his followers where they were. Living with the reality of persecution, these early believers needed to know that God took care of these dimensions of the Spirit.

In verse 13c, John comes back to the children with more reminders. The first mention of "children" is via the word *teknia*, which connotes the dependence or weakness of a young child in relationship to one who is more capable. The second use of children in verse 13c uses the word *paidia*, which emphasizes the subordination or immaturity of the child. Instruction or direction is needed. John reminds his readers that they have received instruction. They were taught, and continue to be taught, regarding their relationship to God as Father (Barker, 320).

The "fathers" are pointed back to 1:1-3, where they are said to regard God and Jesus as one. Also, they are to know that Christ is established as One who has existed from the beginning of creation. These fathers know this truth. They have heard the teaching or preaching of Jesus as fulfillment of the prophesied "messiah." In verse 14, the fathers are reminded that they should know God. As members of the community for some time, they have a responsibility because of this knowledge they possess.

What then of the "young men"? In verse 14b, they are described as "strong." They have emerged victorious in the conflicts of the faith. Twice, they are reminded that they have already lived long enough to overcome "the evil one." We might assume this group consists of people in the church who are not immature in the faith, but are also not advanced in years or life experience. Again, it is best not to assume this title refers to those who are literally young. Rather, it appears that John commends the determined strength of those who have lived the faith for a length of time.

Do Not Love the World

John has now established an idea of the people he addresses in this section. More importantly, he has given them a context for his next teaching. In verse 15, he moves to a practical matter: issuing a warning or application about the awaiting dangers. "Do not love the world or anything in the world," he cautions. I wonder if we are any more poised to receive this teaching than John's New Testament audience.

More than twenty years ago, when I was a college student, a controversial movie was released. Stark and vulgar in its depictions, the film garnered high levels of secular critique. Reporters had a wonderful time with movie critics and viewers alike, all in search of reactions as to whether this movie should play in mainstream theaters. Imagine, then, church leaders' reactions about the movie! My mom asked our wise, aging home-church pastor why he chose not to speak out against the film. He replied simply, "Julie, I learned a long time ago that when a preacher tells people *not* to see a particular movie, he does nothing but sell tickets to that very one!" His answer is more sage advice than wishy-washy copout. Self-restraint, discipline, and a sense of timing are necessary as we live in close proximity to the "world." How can we hear John's wisdom without being drawn toward the curiosity and allure of this "world"? How exactly are we to understand the implications of the term "world"? It will be helpful for your group to spend time discussing these questions.

For now, let us not miss a couple of clarifications on why John made this warning. First, love of the world robs God of our love and attention. Long ago, God proclaimed that he is a "jealous" God (Exod 20:5). With our already finite resources, time, and attention, our love of things other than God takes away from God. Jesus says in Matthew 6:24, "No one can serve two masters; for either he will hate the one and love the other, or he will stand by and be devoted to the one and despise and be against the other. You cannot serve God and mammon." This is the spirit in which John counsels his hearers. We cannot love God and the world equally.

I have known people to take such a statement as a dare. Maybe you have too. Whether it is a conviction that no one else gets to tell them what to do, or an insecurity that yearns to be put to rest, these adults often follow unhealthy impulses. I knew a minister who maintained a low-grade state of church drama that sometimes escalated. Much of this was of his making. He was guided by a dangerous duo: a powerful sense of selfish wishes and a fear about his own lovability that he acted out in a need to prove that he was in charge. When faced with the choice of allowing common sense to prevail or asserting independence, this type of person often chooses to prove himself or herself. Perhaps any of us can be lured toward the wrong choice at times. If mammon for you is not this deep personal sense of independence, then more traditional images might illustrate your distractions from godliness. Pursuit of wealth, status, or power might be what guides you rather than God. Whatever our gods, we are reminded that human spiritual multitasking is not wise. We cannot serve God and mammon.

A second reason behind John's teaching might be that—compared to eternity—the world holds little promise of a future! God's causes are eternal. God's powers are unlimited. God's works are for a lasting goodness and a kingdom that will know no end. Our future with God will not only last for eternity; that future will *be* eternity. As any economic downturn reminds us, we place many of our values in fleeting causes. Our bank accounts and our retirement balances can run empty. Our status can be taken away, or worse, trumped by someone else's. Our preoccupations that seem important can make us obsess over circumstances that don't last the way we thought they might. Even our youth and our health will not last. If we are honest, nothing is lasting when compared with God.

With these cautions in place, we need clarification in order to apply John's wisdom to our lives. Let us revisit this concept of the "world." The use of *kosmos* for world takes place six times in verses 15-17. This is not the same usage of "world" that appears in John 3:16, where we are turned toward God's loving view of all creation. Instead, this depiction in 1 John takes us to a darker place: a world influenced by evil. This world is void and against God. It begins to sound like the chaos that reigned before creation. Verse 16 describes this world, and we are warned against it.

John specifies "the cravings of sinful man, the lust of his eyes, and the boasting of what he has and does." These cravings might literally be the desires of the flesh (*sarkos*). We can understand "flesh" as "the outlook oriented toward self, that which pursues its own ends in self-sufficient independence of God" (Barker, 321). The lust of the eyes could be sexual, but could also be a sense of greed or the allure driven by envy. Are you safe so far? The "pride of life" or "boasting of what he has and does" captures a trouble spot for many of us. This describes an assuming or inconsistent behavior that revels in what one can get or accomplish. Here is where status, power, the want for more stuff, or the will to achieve cause problems. Image and reputation can become gods to us.

Verse 17 is brief enough that it sounds like a summary of previous teachings. We find reiteration that the world and its desires pass away. However, we should acknowledge the rest of the verse before moving on. Much that is in the world is already beginning to pass on. An insurance agent in one of my churches made an observation. He was talking about the degree of denial that guides the transaction even when a client chooses to come and buy an insurance product. He noted that in most of these conversations, the client couches his speech in terms of "in case something happens to me." The agent told me that, when he felt comfortable enough with a client, he interrupted and reminded them, "Oh, something will happen to you. Something will happen to all of us eventually. It's only a matter of what and when." Doctors tell us we are all born into the process of dying. While this may seem like a pessimistic viewpoint, it is also realistic. Much of this world is temporary. The economic meltdown of 2008 reminded us that no companies or individuals are immune to the effects of a global economy grown weak.

A Christian's To-do List

Notice, then, that the writer affirms, "the one who does the will of God lives forever." In his book *Sessions with James*, Michael McCullar wrestled in detail with the tension between faith and works in Christian life. John's phrase may remind many readers of that tension. Is our eternity about works, or is our fate resting on belief in a redeeming Christ? We will likely strain at that theological quagmire—and we should at times. Whatever your outcome, though, John might have a different agenda. He might instead suggest that his point is to steer the listener toward the things of God one more time. While we may wish for a specific warning to avoid failure, John reminds us that faith is not only about a list of *don'ts*. Mature faith is more about a list of *dos*. Self-reliance, lusts of the eyes, and all manner of other sinful engagements won't save us. John wants us in touch with the things that *do* reflect the life and model of Christ. Only obedience to the Lordship of God through Christ brings about lasting life.

We return to the original sense of tension. This tension exists within us as we constantly battle for God to be our guide. In another way, there is tension in the ending note of this text as it speaks to the issue of works versus faith. Perhaps greater still is the tension many of us will experience as we hear Christ say to love the world. Yet, John warns us *not* to love something also called the "world." What will we do with these forces that counter within our spirits? Again, one key is to mature our faith. Through growing in knowledge and experience with God, we will have more resources as we live. By living in touch with others who seem to have godly wisdom, we can learn for ourselves. We can discern the difference between a self-guided investment in sin and a compassionate need to live out loving action toward a creation that is imperfect and flawed this side of heaven.

1. Before studying this text, discuss the "world." Christ has taught us to love the world. John 3:16 says Christ was sent to save the world. Today we will be warned against loving the world! How do you react to these two seemingly contradictory commands?

_____

_____

_____

_____

2. As a child, what did you consider the most important things, events, and possessions in the world? As a teenager? As a young adult? How has your view of these priorities changed over the stages of life?

_____

_____

_____

_____

3. When we refer to something as "worldly," what do we mean? How does living in a "worldly" manner contrast with other types of living?

_____

_____

_____

_____

4. How would you advise a new believer who asked about the balance of living "in" the world but not "of" the world? Discuss this in your group and have someone keep track of responses.

_____

_____

_____

_____

Tension: Do Not Love the World?

5. Somewhere along the way, we must react to John's directive that the "one who does the will of God lives forever." How do you reconcile this teaching with the notion of salvation through the grace of Christ Jesus?

_____

_____

_____

_____

6. In order to process John's warning about not loving the "world," we must acknowledge a list of "don'ts." What would your list of don'ts look like?

_____

_____

_____

_____

7. If we are faithful to John's teaching, then we must mature to a point where we pay attention to life according to Christ-like "dos." What would your list of dos look like?

_____

_____

_____

_____

8. Who in your life helps you want to be a better person, a person more like Christ? Share responses as a group, giving each other a brief description of why this person helps you find a positive balance in living as Christ without "loving the world."

_____

_____

_____

_____

Love: In Deed and in Truth

My favorite consumer-awareness radio show originates here in Atlanta. The host is intelligent, although like anyone else he is not always right. His show broadcasts nationally and offers an amazing source of financial information. Aside from his knowledge, though, what draws me to this particular host is what I perceive as his driving sense of ethic. One of his theories that I often ponder is a core conviction about the nature of big businesses. He holds that there is a corporate thought pattern woven into the American economy. Simply stated, as most companies grow larger, their "brains" grow smaller. Obviously, we could come up with a few exceptions to this pattern. Large companies can keep their functional edge and do perceptive things. But by and large, bureaucracy and groupthink kick in frequently enough that there is credibility to the host's theory. Companies can grow to a point where they begin to exist more to sustain the company than to do the work that serves the customer. When they reach that point, several fronts suffer. Customers lose their use for the company transaction by transaction. Then market share and profitability drop. Stockholders become nervous and begin to react. Soon, the repercussions spread across many sectors.

A well-worn story illustrates this. For a long time, the Swiss were known as the supreme makers of fine watches. Even today, a Swiss-made watch is a fine item to own. But a couple of decades ago, a new technology was developed. Today, most of us wear timepieces that run on quartz technology. These watches are accurate and inexpensive to manufacture. Supposedly, the Swiss were approached first with this breakthrough. As the benchmark of prestigious watchmakers, the Swiss industry largely passed on the opportunity to use quartz technology. Many other companies snatched up the quartz-movement idea, and accurate watches were soon mainstreamed at affordable prices. While heritage and brand recognition remained on the side of many Swiss companies, the watch-buying public reacted decisively. The Swiss lost a large piece of market share, and today they are said to hold much less of market share. The lesson? A case could be made that the established watchmakers forgot that they existed to make accurate timepieces for sale. Instead, they protected their heritage at the cost of their business. I think this is sometimes true of churches and individual Christians.

Too Busy In Jesus' Name?

First John 3:11-24 serves as a reminder to people and churches alike. We can become so busy "doing" the work of church that we lose sight of core values and callings that identify us as "being" church. For John, acts of loving are beacons toward Christ-likeness. Love is like true north on a compass. Love is center-cut evidence of the abiding presence of God. For John, the Christian should never lose the focus of love. Sentimentally, our first reaction might be to wonder why this is even an issue. We would all vote that the call of Christ into "loving" is universal. No one would vote against love. The problem is that we can forget to love. We can become too busy, too distracted, or too important to love, both individually and corporately.

The writer of this letter must have felt that the first-century Christians were losing critical focus. This is a timeless problem for the church. At every stop, I've noticed church members who are busy little Christians. They speak the prevailing "heart language" of the faith. They shop only at Christian businesses and listen only to Christian radio. They are present at every activity—except the missional aspects of church life. These eager hearers of sermons and studiers of the Bible were conspicuously absent when it was time to fill food sacks or drive nails. I have witnessed church bureaucracy slow practiced love to a crawl. Legalism, Bible trivia, congregational management, and internal politics quickly become the danger zones for most church members.

Whereas John has couched some of these writings in contrasts of righteousness and sin, here in 3:11-24 he employs the language of love versus hate. In verse 11, the writer reminds us that the original message continues. He says, "you have heard from the beginning . . . that we should love one another." Note that the word used for "message" was intended as a declaration or an imperative. This is not a suggestion. John sees loving one another as universal and not optional for the genuine Christian. To emphasize his point, he invokes the image of Cain from Genesis 4. John asserts strongly that we are capable of "murder" when love or righteousness is absent.

And They'll Know We Are Christians . . .

In verse 12, "love one another" should remind us of the words of Jesus in John 13:34-35. In the Gospel, Jesus not only issues the "command" to love, but also says love is the identifying quality of his followers. John drives home the point that we do wrong (or neglect to do right!) when we concentrate unduly on ourselves. Left to our natural selves, we are guided by evil or selfish motives. John 8:44 reminds us that Jesus was candid about who we become, apart from the transforming presence of an abiding God. Perhaps today's culture inserts the notion that right and wrong are individual matters of choice. There is much resistance to the notion of a guiding Christian "ethic" today; we support the ethic according to each individual. This contrasts with the identifying benchmark declared by Jesus and affirmed here by 1 John. John says love should guide our decision-making and our living.

Verses 13-15 should catch the attention of individual and gathered Christians alike. In his time, the writer of 1 John says in verse 13, "Do not wonder, brethren, that the world hates you." Today, many of our fellow church members struggle to realize that we do not live in an American culture that is as friendly to the church as it once was. Perhaps the prevailing times never favored the church to the extent it appeared. As far back as the late 1960s, some honest churches began to whisper of a change in generational churchgoing habits. Although the heyday of churchgoing in our country probably extended through the 1970s, clearly a decline is identifiable today. With that decline, many ministers and churches have seen their seats of influence in communities diminish. Church scandals, especially involving money and sex, have cost Christians dearly. Even history is viewed from a more jaded angle, with people building a case that the church has done more damage than good in the name of Christ through war, conquest, and discrimination. In an increasingly secular society, some even generally "hate" the church.

We might be surprised to discover different reasons the church and Christians are less than popular. John speaks to assurance and honest identity in verse 14. He begins by saying we can "know that we have passed out of death into life because we love the brethren." In contrast, though, "He who does not love remains in death." It is easy to reason that the church might be frowned upon for its human foibles. Many resent us because we sometimes fail to measure up to Christ's standards. But there is another surprising angle to why the world might hate Christians who are supposed to love. We must be honest about the various human reactions to love. Many times, love inspires more love and goodness. Good deeds bring out more good deeds.

To the truly evil-hearted, though, the presence of love conjures a guilt-driven anger. Doing good in Christ's name irritates those less inclined to live like Christ. Hear John's observation through these filters: "Do not wonder, brethren, that the world hates you." If love means health and growth, then the absence of love brings about decay. In a consumer-driven culture that is perhaps growing more selfish, the presence of love makes many uncomfortable. Verse 15 continues to make the case that God's abiding love cannot yield hate. It is likely that people who knew precisely who he was, rather than enemies who did not understand him, executed Christ.

Called toward Loving Acts

In verses 16-18, John reiterates the prescription. We cannot be responsible for the whims of a selfish culture. We cannot give in to our own natures. Nor can we throw our hands in the air and worry about negative reactions to being Christian. One could say, "Well, they hate us for being imperfect, and they hate us when we get it right!" John does not flinch. Verse 16 marches on by reminding us that Christ gave his all to a fickle world. I wonder who was in the crowd calling for the release of Barabbas, when earlier they had waved palm branches and declared Jesus' triumphant entry as the coming of a king: "By this we know love, that he laid down his life for us; and we ought to lay down our lives for the brethren." Just as Jesus has done, so must we do also. The use of "love" here is an imperative form. It is absolute and refers back to a past revelation that John's reader should have known. Thus, the phrase "he laid down his life for us" simply ensures that the reader doesn't miss the tie to Christ himself.

If Christ did so, "we ought to lay down our lives for the brethren," John reasons. Christ's absolute form of love is so unmistakable that one African woman is said to have responded to her first Christian missionary sermon with, "There! I always told you that there ought to be a God like that" (Wilder and Hoon, 263–64). In addition to being compelled by Christ to love, there is a moral component to our need to love. Verse 16 couches our responsibility not only as an act of obedience, but as an "ought." We are not only bound to love; we are called toward acts of loving. As Christ would have compassion upon need, so are we led to respond in helpful ways to those who need us.

Verses 17-18 bring into play a proof of love. That is, if we have resources and capability, then we are compelled to respond by sharing them. If God's love truly abides in one of us, then we are called to give what we have in order to better those around us. According to John, without loving action, there is reason to wonder if God is present in us at all. Or, to our church-addicted brothers or sisters, "let us not love in word or speech, but in deed and in truth." Paul's words in 1 Corinthians 13 should come to mind here. Karl Marx is thought to have said that the Church of England of his day would more readily pardon an attack upon one of its thirty-nine Articles of Religion than upon one thirty-ninth of its income (Wilder and Hoon, 264).

Verse 19 begins another pastoral effort to assure his people. Of course, he also wants to correct distorted and damaging behavior in the church. John wants believers to be freed by certainty. No doubt he finds that the desire for certainty could be a driving influence toward better living. In verse 20, John acknowledges that there will be doubt in the presence of God ". . . whenever our hearts condemn us, for God is greater than our hearts and he knows everything." He continues in verse 21 by making a powerful observation: the guilty or condemned heart is of less use to the kingdom. We have all known the person whose core attitude is, "Why bother trying to be good if I'm just going to fail?" Like Winnie the Pooh's perpetually down friend, we take up the voice of Eeyore and wonder why we should bother trying to live like Christ. It seems that all we see is failure among God's people to measure up. John asserts that if we live lives of love, then our hearts are not as likely to condemn us. (See Paul's work in Romans 5:1-5.) Without condemnation, we have confidence before God.

With verse 22, John shifts to another reason for confidence in loving. When we are in tune with the heart of God, our prayers reflect it. John suggests that we "receive from him whatever we ask, because we keep his commandments." Many pluck words like these from Scriptures and carry them around like a genie's bottle. They rub that figurative promise and petition God for their heart's desire. Of course, the risk of deep and confusing disappointment comes with this type of faith. John's assertion here is more reliable if we hear it as an affirmation of how our prayers will reflect the desires of God in the first place. We are not as likely to ask for riches, impossible outcomes, or frivolous goods when an abiding God guides us. We are not as distracted and gullible when we keep God's commandments. John 15:7 captures this same Johannine mindset as we hear, "If you abide in me, and my words abide in you, ask whatever you will, and it shall be done for you." Jesus would not intend to fool us about prayer. This is as corrective as it is an open-ended promise. Still, there is assurance when we frame it in its intended light.

What are these "commandments" that we are to keep? In his closing thoughts, John specifies. Verse 23 says we are to "believe on the name of his Son Jesus Christ, and love one another." This is the imperative laid down by Jesus himself. Not that loving one another is easy. The church has perhaps failed in making the tasks of love, forgiveness, truth, and righteousness sound too simple. These are not sentiments that happen by the flip of a switch. There is an old saying that the road to hell is paved with good intentions. Likewise, if we are honest, our belief is not always easy, either. We have doubts, and we must hang our faith on a framework of unanswerable mysteries. Again, many Christians do not reward honesty about those dimensions of our faith. They prefer black-and-white answers that eventually fail under the strain of life. However, John closes by pulling the reader back toward these commands to believe and to love anyway.

In verse 24, John summarizes by stubbornly adhering to his convictions. If we keep these commandments we abide in God. Conversely, God surely abides in us. By this, John says, we will find assurance that we are God's children. In John 6:29, belief in Christ is represented as a "work of God" in itself. This work of God is commanded of Christians, but we are not weighted down without help. The term used for "work" is the type that utilizes assistance (Wilder and Hoon, 271). Thus, in verse 24, mention of the Spirit of God reminds us that we live far from alone here on earth. The encouragement of verse 23 to believe, then, rewards us with the assurance in verse 24. First John drives the reader with a hard assignment. Faithful loving and action is not easy. As I remind my young adult learners occasionally, Christ himself was killed for living the lifestyle we are called to take up. I don't believe many of his followers died of natural causes either. To live as Christ exacts a cost at times. Living counter to the prevailing culture, even in a more positive manner than others, sometimes isolates the believer. Still, John says, we must practice love in deed and in truth. Then we will know of the abiding presence of God.

1. What do you believe makes a "Christian" unique from others in the world? From other "good" people in the world?

_____

_____

_____

_____

2. What might be a way to understand the differences between "believing," "doing," and "being"? How do these three realities differ?

_____

_____

_____

_____

3. This chapter includes an illustration about Swiss watchmakers. Using the principle of that story, what might be the church's blind spot? In what ways might we lose our focus from time to time?

_____

_____

_____

_____

4. When the church loses focus, what are typical excesses or distractions that cause this to happen?

_____

_____

_____

_____

Love: In Deed and in Truth

5. When you hear, "He who does not love remains in death," what meaning do you draw? How can this be so?

_____
_____
_____
_____

6. Among the other teachings, our text indicates that we may ask for whatever we desire and it will be given. In light of your life experience, how are we to hear this?

_____
_____
_____
_____

7. If we are destined to fail, what is our incentive for trying to live as John suggests?

_____
_____
_____
_____

8. This chapter suggests that the act of believing is in itself a work of God. In other words, one of the realities is that we will have to work at believing. How does that fit with what you've been taught? How might this be a helpful insight?

_____
_____
_____
_____

8 Assurance: Loving One Another

1 Jn 4:7-21

The words from 1 John 4 speak in practical detail about the nature of God's intention of love. Consider reading the entire chapter to prepare for this session. While 1 Corinthians 13 is better known as the "love chapter" of the Bible, this discussion by John rivals that passage for clarity and specifics. These words speak of a love so powerful that God must surely be its source. John also gives us a bonus: this brand of love is so powerful that we should find assurance as we experience it and offer it, assurance about our relationship with God and God's nearness to us for eternity.

The Many Loves of a Lifetime

What are some things you love? Well documented in our language is that we use the same word to connote many differing levels of fondness. I love to walk around in the old city of Prague. I love to go to Atlanta Braves' games. I love good, well-prepared food. Begrudgingly, I admit that I love our cat. Happily, I'll bore you with all the ways I love my wife! Not even knowing me, you can detect differing levels of importance for each of these in my life. Or can you?

At this point in your study, what are some things you love? Go ahead; it's safe. This is not a setup so that I can make you feel bad later in the study. I hope you'll talk freely with your study group about the things you "love" in life. Celebrate these and get to know one another better in the process. We *should* have strong feelings about many things in God's wonderful world. Inspiration and advances help improve life. Humans have a part in creating some of the wonder and beauty we see. These are not bad things. They are not without meaning and import. No doubt, though, you will notice different levels of priority in the things you discuss.

Such an exercise is not merely about our struggle to use a word correctly. One way to understand God's need to redeem us is to admit that we struggle to understand the many loves in our lives. We confuse the importance of our various loves in relation to God. Some of them become little gods to us in our daily living. We should probably ask ourselves, "What is it to 'love'?" I hope your group is willing to engage such an abstract concept and discuss meaningfully what "loving" something or someone entails. What do we do when we love? What does love say? What results from love?

Any discussion of this text from 1 John 4 is without context if we do not honor the words of verses 1-6. In many ways, they echo themes studied elsewhere in this book. In those sentences, John reminds the reader that false teachers abound. There is danger in following them. Sooner or later, we must test what we believe in order to know the difference between false teachings and those of Christ. Consider reading these first six verses and keeping them in mind as you hear the words of the main text. John speaks briefly, but boldly, about testing what we believe. From there, John moves us toward our focus for this study that begins with verse 7.

At my house, we like movies that end well. I'll admit we prefer movies with happy endings. As sure as I could begin naming movies, someone would take offense to one of them. Such a list isn't necessarily intended for general play at your church (or even for your family), but more for illustrating the point. We've enjoyed romantic comedies or musicals that end well. *Mamma Mia* is a recent release that comes to mind. *Love, Actually, Notting Hill,* and *You've Got Mail* also offer happy endings. Among other themes, these movies explore human dimensions of what it means to love in healthy (and unhealthy) ways. John points us toward relational and spiritual health. We are called to love in ways only made possible by the life and model of Christ, in ways Hollywood scriptwriters rarely portray. This New Testament way of love is beyond sentimental. This love is beyond even the level of commitment. In John's portrayal, we love because God has already loved. Sometimes this love flies in the face of logic or even conventional possibility.

But How Can We Know?

In this session, we explore John's conviction about "assurance" in our faith. John rests on the end result of healthy love. Or, depending on how you view his words, he presents healthy love as an indicator of our salvation and renewal. Either way, we should sense another connection between these letters and the Gospel according to John. Love is the happy ending that emerges when people of God live by faith. This is a kingdom indicator that should produce more than merely good moments. We should feel a sense of assurance from living as Christ lived.

How can "love" give assurance? In some big-picture way, John's call to love may demonstrate salvation. As we are transformed and renewed, it becomes more and more possible to live as Christ lived. Can someone live nicely without following Christ? Sure they can. Are healthful relationships exclusively limited to Christians? Of course not. But for most of us, we should feel some assurance as we realize that we can live in ways that might have seemed impossible before we chose to follow Christ as Lord of our lives.

Several basic questions might help us get deeper into the discussion of New Testament "love": Is it easier to straighten each other out than to love each other? Why is God's great love for us a truth worth pondering every day? Is it possible to love God and not love others? Is it possible to love others and not love God? Questions like this cause us to treat love as more than a mere descriptive word or emotional state. God's type of love is more versatile than a particular word or pit-of-the-stomach feeling; it is complete.

Let's explore some background for the passage. First, as mentioned earlier, either the apostle John or one of his helpers wrote this passage around AD 100. The early church had spread to outlying provinces. To many scholars, this letter seems to have come from Ephesus, and it is Greek in style and substance. By this time, the church was largely Gentile, so the task of interpreting Christianity to a Greek-thinking world was upon the early believers.

This passage involves *theology*, the study of God. It nudges the reader a step closer to God, offering instruction that tells us about God's expectations, how God has designed life to work, and what is good and right. We can react to these words on many levels. In theological study, we ponder how the transactions of love work between God and humans. Thus, what the passage leaves unanswered will likely send us into further reflection and study.

Additionally, we can view this passage as an *ethical* teaching. Specifically, this passage establishes the centrality of living like Christ in obedience to the Lordship of God. Our behavior, our treatment of others, our decision-making—these ethical drivers must all arise out of our belief. This is not the type of text that feeds the self-centered wants of a consumer Christian. Instead, the teachings clearly turn believers toward others in quality interaction, all on behalf of a loving, abiding God.

John's words in this text are also *definitional* in nature. We learn about God's intent through this text and gain further insight into who Christ was among us. Of course, rather than reading these words as a heartwarming experience, we gain definition about who we are also designed to become. John first commends love, more so than he speculates about God. John reminds his audience that to follow God is to live a life of love. For him, these notions of salvation and love are inseparable. John sees love as the natural extension of faith in Christ, an expected result of Christ's saving us. But biblical readers encounter the underlying question, "What is God like?"

The Greeks, a wise, beautiful, and powerful people, worshiped many gods. They highly valued reason and would have debated new ideas of any kind in the city's marketplace. The Christians' one God was more up-close and accessible than the often cruel gods worshiped by the Greeks. In contrast to his Hebrew background, Jesus Christ came as a new covenant of God. As such, John reminds his readers that this God is loving. This same God is an active presence in our lives, not a foreboding observer standing by ready to correct! This God patiently and constantly acts for the good among humanity.

The Essence of God

The word "love" is used twenty-five times in verses 6-21. Perhaps this seems obvious, but such concentrated usage indicates that love is a central idea for John. However, as definitional as this is, the reader needs to maintain perspective. In the face of John's message, we can take on an overbalanced notion about God. While love is a good word to define God, it is not the only word for describing God. God is many other powerful realities for all of creation. Even so, John feels an urgency to express that God is love.

Many of us have experienced enforced emotions. That is, our parents ordered us to make up with a playmate or family member as they refereed a dispute. For instance, mom or dad told us to apologize. Through clenched teeth, we muttered, "I'm sorry," just to get by. No one was convinced, but we met the requirement. Not so with John. For all his emphasis on love, in 3:18 and 4:9 John explains the action behind the word "love." In so doing, John moves beyond the words of love and even beyond the attitude or the intention of love. John is clearly talking about a practice of love. Human love is a reflection of something in the divine nature itself. It does not begin in us. John recognizes that humankind is not in itself loving. In verse 7, John stakes his claim perhaps against the pre-Gnostic movement. Especially here, he makes clear that all who know and follow God share in the calling and knowledge of love's power.

Most of us have no qualms with John's words about love in this letter. That is, until perhaps verse 8: "He who does not love does not know God; for God is love." This is a troublesome verse because the language suggests that the person who does not love has not yet begun to know God. We all know the sour, mean-spirited person at church or in our families, or we catch ourselves being the mean-spirited ones. We are all capable of being less than loving. For John, one *can* love without God but is *not as likely* to love. Similarly, here, with the absence of love comes the likelihood of the absence of God. John likely intended this verse to be a more positive thought than it sounds to our ears. That is, we can know God and fail to love, but we are less likely to fail when we're in the presence of God. If God is love, then, when we are transformed through our acceptance and salvation, we become more like the essence of that loving God.

The words of verses 9-10 should be familiar to the reader. Specifically, John 3:16 might come to mind: "This is how God showed his love among us: He sent his one and only Son into the world that we might live through him. This is love: not that we loved God, but that he loved us and sent his Son as an atoning sacrifice for our sins." Beginning with 1 John 4:7, this section discusses what you may know as God's love (*agapē*) rather than brotherly love (*eros*). John's distinction helps clarify the matter. God's love is assumed to be a gift only bestowed upon the Christian follower. This love goes beyond fellowship or good intent. It chooses to be made manifest, at times in the face of other wills that might seem sensible. This love is stubborn and determined and denotes an act of the will under the direction of God. Jesus' teaching of love for enemies (Matt 5:43-48) is a good illustration (McDowell, 214–15). First John 4:10 speaks to the mysterious transaction of God sending a Son out of "love" for creation. Verses 11 and 12 make the case for the necessity of love and for the testimony found in God's kind of love among people. While we may not directly experience the presence of God, God's kind of love indicates the guidance of the holy presence within us. For John's audience, this was a new thought. Our Christian faith actually changes values and relationships beyond the legalism accepted for generations as the fulfillment of the "obligation" with God.

John reestablishes the "abiding" nature of God in verses 13-21. Whether couched in terms of the Spirit or of salvation, God is "in" the believer. Verse 13 uses the verbs for "knowing" and "living" (or "abiding") to suggest ongoing action rather than a moment in time (Smalley, 249). Verse 14 is another response to the pre-Gnostic movement, as John states, "we have seen and testify that the Father has sent his Son as Savior of the world." In verse 15, confession is included in the saving act of submitting to God's abiding love. Verses 16-17 speak again about reassurance. First, we're reminded that God's love abiding in us must suggest that we are God's. Then, verse 17 goes to the transaction of God's love being "perfected" in us; we have confidence for a day of judgment because God's love is only available to "us" (believers). When we consider the matter, that good news is still sobering. God's kind of love is the subject here, not just the occasional loving act of a friendly or romantic person.

In verse 18, John addresses the subject of fear. For too long, many churches have asserted that fear or doubt has no place in the life of the "true" believer. John's words here don't seem to help us at first glance. The reality is that most of us will have periods of doubt throughout our Christian journeys. Here, John tries to reassure his first-century audience. In so doing, he contributes something for us all. In this verse, John makes the bold assertion that there is "no" fear in perfected love. That perfected love, of course, is the type of love given us by an abiding God. John suggests that fear relates to punishment. Instead of fearing, the believer should feel assured by the presence of God. Today, we might suggest that John is coaching or assuring. It is confusing for us to hear John say there is an absence of fear in perfected love. Some scholars believe John might have indicated the capacity of perfected love. That is, God's type of love is capable of casting out fear. Your study group may offer various perspectives of this verse as it has applied to their Christian journeys.

Verse 19 establishes once gain the *agapē* love as a gift from God. This verse indicates an order to life; God has loved us *first*. Because we have accepted this abiding God into who we are, we are then capable of loving in the way that God has loved us. In fact, we are capable of loving both ourselves and others as God has loved us, and we are called to do so. In verse 20, John clears confusion by reversing the message. If one claims to love but then lives in a way that demonstrates the opposite, that person is a "liar." This is an extension of John's earlier case, for God is incapable of hating. If God has transformed the true believer, then he or she will not only voice love but will deliver *agapē* love. Verse 21 simply affirms that living a life of love is a "commandment." We are neither suggested nor hinted toward loving. We cannot claim the abiding presence of a saving God without living as God instructed us to live

Here, then, is a problem. If our love reflects something from the divine parent, and if children normally look a bit like the parent, then what about the times when we misbehave, disagree, or mistreat each other in our churches? (See 4:20-21.) This capacity to hurt fellow believers is troubling in its implication about us. Here is one possibility, though: we will reflect God's love, but will fail often enough to recall that love does not originate in us. Still, the commandment is held in front of us as the standard, even if we know we cannot reach that level of perfection.

Here is the jumping off place for most of us. If these verses in 1 John 4 speak about a love that originates in God, then how can we be capable of delivering on the commitment? Try as we may, we go into faith knowing we will sometimes fail. For many, the real question becomes, "Why should I even try?" John seems to suggest that when we are truly transformed, we can do no other than try. Attached to this commitment is hope. John also suggests that, at times, an abiding God will enact surprising love from inside us. We will love beyond ourselves because God works to transform us beyond our capacities as humans. Occasionally, as we see God's Spirit at work, we should feel comforted or assured.

1. What are some things you love? Share openly in the group and learn more about each other.

_____

_____

_____

_____

2. What is it to "love"? What do we do when we love? What does love say? What results from love?

_____

_____

_____

_____

3. Read the following statements and ask for "agree/disagree" responses. Allow for discussion.
• It is easier to straighten each other out than to love each other.
• God's great love for us is a truth worth pondering every day.
• It is impossible to love God and not love others.
• It is impossible to love others and not love God.

4. What practices do you need in order to grow into living the kind of love John challenges us to live?

_____

_____

_____

_____

5. What practices do you need in order to develop a lifestyle that helps you "abide" in God (and one that allows God to abide in you)?

_____

_____

_____

_____

6. What does it mean practically for us to "love"?

_____

_____

_____

_____

7. How can we love in our workplaces? How can we love while driving? How can we love while at Wal-Mart? How can we love at a yard sale? According to 1 John, why should we love in these places?

_____

_____

_____

_____

8. When you love others, how should they receive your love? Ultimately, do their responses affect whether you should love or not?

_____

_____

_____

_____

9. Author and leader Bo Prosser is known for saying, "People go where they know they are prepared for and will be cared for." What does this have to do with "love" as 1 John teaches?

_____

_____

_____

_____

Deception: Look to Yourselves

What is truth? Though the pages of this study guide may outlive any cultural whim, these words are written during an odd time with regard to "truth." In these days, many seem to view truth as a moving target. Rather than being comfortable with the existence of absolute or generalized truths, individuals are afforded the luxury of arriving at their own customized truth. There is "my" truth, and there is "your" truth. You need not feel constrained to see my truth, only to seek your own. Of course, this leaves tremendous room not only for disagreement but also for wandering in search of truth but finding little substance to which we can tether our souls. This is yet another accommodation to a consumer-oriented society that is fearsome about making commitments.

So Really—What *Is* Truth?

Therefore, when Christians claim to have found truth in Christ, others find their claims problematic. I talked with a young father who was experiencing marital difficulty. Among the myriad troubles was a spiritual issue. His wife forbade him to involve the children in church, since she feared that her children would be taught a theology of personal "sin." Personally, the wife was not willing to accept this truth of Christian faith. While some have had the competent responsibility of coming to their own faith for centuries, sharing tried and true insights of faith is now viewed as more suspect than perhaps in the past. This brings a couple of challenges to hearing the words of 2 John.

This brief, thirteen-verse collection asserts that a charge of deception has been worked among the believers. Yesterday's deception is today's alternate, or personal, truth. If all truths are equally valid, then how can the notion of deception exist? Or evil and wrongdoing, for that matter? Second, like many of the writings before, this letter claims Jesus Christ is the very truth that is eternal. That is, this letter claims more than truth *about* Christ. Christ *himself* is viewed as being the truth upon which all other truths are evaluated.

The "Elder" who writes this letter is of some interest. Presumably, the title was familiar to the parties involved, even if it's a bit of a mystery to readers today. A more transliterated understanding of the word might be "Presbyter," which sounds like a position but indicates that the writer is an older person. In usage, the term has also seemed to connote a leader or a person with authority.

Apart from the assumption that there is indeed Truth (Jesus Christ) and also the possibility of deception, this letter might have little value. The writer stakes his claims on several realities that he sees as trustworthy, but he is convinced of both assumptions and more. First, John seems to subscribe to the notion that the church is sacred. His greeting is addressed to the "Elect Lady." One might wonder if this were written to an individual person. Another possibility is that John wrote this letter to one church. Scholars seem to view the latter as more likely. If the church is personified, then how is the meaning understood? Much as the title "Bride of Christ" reflects God's love for the gathered church, "elect" bestows a sacred trust to the church as well. The closing verse from 2 John sends to the recipient greetings from the "children of your elect sister." In other biblical texts, both Israel and Jerusalem receive feminine personification. This seems to be one church greeting another. These titles show a serious, yet precious understanding of the church. Unlike 1 John, which was written to a broader audience, it appears that 2 John was sent from one local body to another.

An Abiding Truth

Next, the reader finds evidence that these churches share a bond. John expresses love toward a group that also enjoys an abiding truth. The concept of God's "abiding truth" sounds so good to our longing ears that we can miss an important statement. In verse 2, John declares that the "truth" abides in us. D. Moody Smith writes that these claims are in fact fairly "typical Johannine language." These standard ingredients of love, truth, knowledge, and abiding all express powerful beliefs about God, however. "Truth" for this

Johannine community is Christ (Smith, 140). While some may focus solely on the nature of this truth, we should consider the phrase in verse 2 that suggests this truth "abides in us and will be with us forever." This should remind us of John's Gospel (14:15-17) where the disciples are promised a Spirit of truth that will dwell in them. Old Testament prophets also foretold of a time when God's word would be sealed in the hearts of believers. In 2 Corinthians 3, Paul alludes to this notion of a living word written in the hearts of believers.

In all, the word "truth" occurs in the first four verses of 2 John. Not only is Jesus understood as this eternal truth, but it seems that those who follow the gospel have that truth. In fact, they embody the truth and are bound by the common Spirit. Some suggest that the Apostolic Creed finds much of its power in texts like this, as the catholic church now comes into view. Did you ever trip over that particular segment while reciting the beautiful creed? I was well into adulthood before I allowed myself to say the word "catholic" aloud. Finally I understood that I was not being disloyal to my Baptist heritage, since the concept of the unified (catholic) church in Christ is a different concept from the large group we refer to as Roman Catholics with a capital "C."

From verse 4 on, we gain better insight into the problem that 2 John may have addressed. That "some" of the elect's children are following the truth implies that others are not. Verse 5 further reminds readers that the greatest commandment is to "love." For the law-minded, John couches the admonition toward love as a primary commandment. Some were still inclined to view following commandments, Old Testament style, as equal with loving God. Then John reminds them that they are commanded to love one another, and Christ showed us how to live in that way. That is (v. 6), following love is the same as following a commandment. This is the life and nature of Christ.

I have a friend who jokingly refers to her life as a "happy bubble." Although she is wise and grounded, she works hard to look at life on the bright side. Where victory or hope is possible, she will try to find it. However, when she lives in the happy bubble, it is because of legitimate good. There are those, however, who are simply naïve. Their happy bubbles are constructed of denial and a lack of self-awareness. John paints a balanced picture for us in this letter. On the one hand, he espouses the Christly good found in love and truth. He believes in his soul that this way of living is in keeping

Deception: Look to Yourselves

with the model of our Lord. On the other, he is clear that not all is good and trustworthy in this life. In verse 7, John tells the reader that many deceivers have gone out, and that these deceivers specifically deny that Christ has taken on flesh. For all his talk of truth, love, and mercy, John is blunt about these persons. He calls them the antichrist. If they are convincing enough, if they are appealing and speak loudly enough, their message will catch on. John knows this about people.

John's view of the "coming of Christ" is also timeless. We should not overlook his use of the present tense. No one would have faulted John for couching this phrase in past tense, indicating that Christ came. But his emphasis is not limited in time. Although Christ came at one moment in time, the language used here communicates ongoing action. This is to remind us that the coming of Christ continues to provide presence and redemption for all generations who might choose to believe (Smalley, 229–30).

Knowing What We Believe

Then, as now, dealing with false messengers begins with knowing what you yourself believe. Without such understanding, one cannot filter well enough to distinguish the absence of truth from the living truth. Thus, this small letter turns with the eighth verse. That is, John prescribes that the people "look to yourselves" so they might not lose what they—the church—have worked for. What is at stake? John's response is that there is a "full reward."

In stating that survivors must know what they believe, then what might John think is central to an empowering faith? We can draw some elements from his writings in this letter. Even the problem of not acknowledging the coming of Christ communicates one crucial element. The believer needs to accept that God has in fact taken on human flesh and walked among us. This we gain from verse 7. If we know we are to follow the model of Christ in our lives, then verse 3 adds a life practice of grace, mercy, and peace to the qualities that embody our faith. Moving now from verse 9, we find that a "doctrine" of Christ himself is specifically mentioned, that is, Christ as more than a historical reference or merely a human who was good. To believe in a "doctrine of Christ" is to hold the Son in deeper regard. John offers that a true disciple transforms his or her life by believing so as to become like Christ. People faith live like Christ because they trust that this is what God intended: believing not only in concept about Christ, but practicing and "carrying" the doctrine of Christ in our lives.

Are we finished with the deception motif? Not quite. John warns the believers of his day that they must do more than just believe correctly. They must have better than good intentions. When I was a little boy, motels were all the rage. The interstate system was still under construction, but already the chain-run corporate motel began popping up along the highways. One brand in particular had a noticeable color scheme and layout to its signage. Our family tended to use this brand of motel, and staying in one meant we were doing something special. We were on a trip! Any time I spotted one from the road, I pointed to the sign and begged my parents to pull in. Even if we had just gotten on our way from the last motel, the sign was enough to make me ready to check in to the next one. My parents patiently explained that we hadn't yet arrived at our next destination. It seems that in the time of John's second letter, honorable travelers did not stay in inns by the roadside. Many believe inns were collecting places for crooks and shady types in general. Travelers going to visit church groups stayed in homes instead. Often that meant the home of a stranger or, at best, the home of an acquaintance of an acquaintance.

The early church had a quandary about their ministry of hospitality. On the one hand, Christ taught them to love and honor even the stranger who might need a place to sleep. On the other hand, when these people hosted someone, even a stranger, they were seen as becoming a part of whatever business that individual's journey might include. By the mere act of taking the person in, one became linked with that person as a supporter. John speaks to this in verses 10-11. He clearly warns the true Christian believer against becoming a supporter of that which is deceptive. This includes not even taking questionable people into the house as guests.

Today, one problem I occasionally have with church members is that all things labeled "Christian" sound good to them. Store shelves are stocked with "Christian" things I would rather my members not read and embody. Organizations and web sites teach and indoctrinate ideas inconsistent with our church's practice of Christianity. Yet all of them say they are Christian, and may even intend to be Christian. In our culture of respect and openness, this is particularly problematic. One could ask, "What is the harm in your members reading and experimenting a little? Don't you trust them?" My answer would be, "I trust the ones who truly know what they believe. I trust those who know how to listen to what others are saying and discern their message." Otherwise, I don't like for them even to "receive them into the house . . . or give any greeting." This is the same teaching that 2 John contributes. What I am saying, and what John is saying, sounds narrow-minded to many. One might again ask, "Who appointed you God?" I would have to reply, "No one. But I was appointed at least to shepherd." Even for us, John's words ring timeless, but they are troubling words to those who feel boxed in by the call to discernment.

If we are not to greet and receive those who carry deception, how likely is it that we will usher them into positions of leadership? Or allow them to become teachers or trainers in our churches? Or to follow closely their television ministries, subscribe to their newsletters, send money that belongs to our local churches, or click habitually on their web sites? John issues fair warnings that what might seem open-minded to some is quite dangerous to most.

Still Not Satisfied?

Does it seem like what you read in 2 John does not reflect a high trust level in the reader? That is where the gathered body, the church, comes in. Let us travel back to what is perhaps John's central thought in this letter. In verse 8, he teaches that to counter deception, "Look to yourselves." Large groups are capable of being wrong, and the majority does not always make the right judgment call. Even so, the body is still our best chance to discern what is pure. The local church is responsible for holding on to the doctrine of Christ. Do you need help dealing with questionable belief? The resources you need to make a Christ-like decision may be standing around you in your congregation. Does it sound like Christ? Does it act like Christ? Really? Look to yourselves and see!

Be careful, though. At times, like a small child, the church is drawn to pretty people and shiny trinkets. As I write, I recently had a conversation with a young colleague in ministry. We talked about the church's pattern of appointing unlikely, sometimes unfit leaders. I reminded him that, to quote that popular bumper sticker, the world is "run by those who show up." Humility, relational openness, brotherly or sisterly compassion, servanthood, justice, and ethical practice: these are the things of Christ. They reflect the presence of Christ in believers. To add to the confusion, *all* of us are flawed and will disappoint each other at times. Still, we can watch the tests of time. We can read and listen for the character of Christ to be present, but we have to know what we believe about Christ. We have to be willing to think, pray, and put forth effort. Sadly, many Christians are simply not up for this adventurous and discerning journey. They are, as Isaiah 57 warns, subject to their misplaced open-mindedness being blown about in the wind.

John closes with a personal word of warmth. He says he would like to say much more to these fellow believers. Perhaps he ran out of time in writing this particular letter. Perhaps his urgency to send them these words demanded that he economize and get the letter on its way. Whatever the limit, John makes it clear that the extent of his concern for them is not fully addressed here. There is more love, more faith, more hope to talk about, but he will count on a chance to be with them face to face, where he is not limited by print.

He holds the hope of seeing their faces and fellowshipping with them in person. He wants to hear their voices and touch their hands of hospitality with Christ's truth. Let us not miss one final lesson: the church is a unique fellowship. Verses 12-13 are more than kind closing thoughts. Those who believe in the Bride of Christ still have an understanding she is different. She gives us a dimension that we cannot have alone. That is, we participate in the life of the church so that "our joy may be complete." Though we are isolated in today's unique consumer culture, we cannot replace the sense of richness and belonging found in God's church. We can't find the fullness of the church by watching a service on television. We can't find the fullness of the church by participating in the latest online social network. We can't even find the fullness of the church in Bible study. The Bride of Christ is a living body made up of imperfect humans who are trying to follow Christ. John writes in order to strengthen the church so that you and I may have a place to become strong.

1. What is "truth"? We live in an age in which people have a different understanding of truth. Discuss what the word "truth" brings to mind in your group.

_____

_____

_____

_____

2. Why might the Christian faith need established truths as believers attempt to practice a gathered faith as the church?

_____

_____

_____

_____

3. If all persons' truths are viewed as equally valid, then how can the notion of deception exist? Or evil and wrongdoing, for that matter?

_____

_____

_____

_____

4. How does John's Gospel (14:15-17) inform our reading of 2 John? (Specifically consider where the disciples are promised a Spirit of truth that will dwell in them.)

_____

_____

_____

_____

5. How does obedience through a lifestyle of "love" differ from the Old Testament concept of following the Law? After all, both are biblical patterns of being faithful to God.

_____

_____

_____

_____

6. In today's mass media marketplace, scores of books, web sites, and television shows are labeled as "Christian." However, John would remind us that not all that is called Christian is actually of Christ. How can we know the difference?

_____

_____

_____

_____

7. John warns against greeting, fellowshipping with, or hosting false teachers. Do you think there is any danger for most believers in what seems like simple, open-minded dialogue with those who differ?

_____

_____

_____

_____

8. As exemplified in the call for the crucifixion of Christ, even the large group isn't always right! How can the gathered church work together to ensure that Christ-like wisdom prevails? Be specific as you discuss.

_____

_____

_____

_____

Fellowship: Imitate What Is Good!

Imitation as Adults?

Who have you imitated during your life? When I was a kid, I wanted to be like Batman. And Daniel Boone. And Superman—but mostly Batman. That's who I copied when I was a kid. Not the comic book heroes, either. The television ones! These shows aired as original episodes back in the 1950s and 1960s. Some of you remember. My brother and I rushed to get homework done so we could watch them!

How do you play the role of one of these characters? If it's Batman, you need a cape: a bath towel safety-pinned around your neck and hanging down. You also needed a utility belt like what Batman and Robin wore. They kept all sorts of gadgets in the belts that they could use to rescue themselves from trouble and to round up the bad guys. As young boys, we collected random items and hauled them around with us just in case one of the cows or pigs on our farm fell victim to a super criminal.

My brother and I got a large hinge at our dad's store and attached a long, thin rope to it. Maybe we dreamed of using it to throw our "Bat hook" onto a roof and climb the building. I think we're lucky we didn't put a window out with that thing. Or, if we decided to play on the frontier of Boonesborough, a small pine tree chopped down and cleaned made a nice "musket" to carry around. We tried to be quiet and practiced walking stealthily through the woods. I think we managed to sneak up on our fifteen-year-old cat one time. He was deaf and half-blind, of course.

But viewpoints change. Once we grow up, we don't like to admit to imitating anyone! We're taught to establish our own identity, to be our own people and chart our own courses. This ought to render the philosophical possibility of "cultural trends" obsolete for adults, except there are fads and trends among people of all ages! Maybe it means, in some ways, that we never really stop imitating.

Some in the fairly controversial field of "mematics" have argued that imitation makes humans unique among animals. Imitation might be a key in human history because those who were good at it had a wider arsenal of learned cultural behavior at their disposal, such as tool making or even language. *Imitation*—when we use that word with regard to leather, we picture something we bought on Canal Street in New York. If we speak of imitation wood, we picture furniture that is not built of top-quality materials. If it's a document or a signature that's stamped rather than hand-signed, we picture a fake. Imitation = of less value!

In our Scripture, though, we hear that imitation is good for the fellowship. John commends the believers for extending hospitality to the "brethren," because with these brethren came a "truth." That "truth" is good to follow. One commentary said, "The Elder's encouragement to imitate good reminds us that we need a living example more than we need verbal nudges for healthy living" (Wilder and Hoon, 311). Indeed, Daniel Webster is to have said that the strongest argument he knew for the existence of God was an aunt of his who lived in the hills of Vermont.

Gaius apparently excelled in this gift of hospitality, even though these men were strangers to him. Many of us have likely underestimated the New Testament encouragement to practice hospitality. The Greek word literally means "love for strangers." Too many of us think hospitality means we buy chips and salsa and invite our friends over to watch Monday Night Football. I'm in favor of watching football with your friends, but that's not what biblical hospitality is all about. True hospitality involves opening your heart and home to those in need. It means sharing your time and resources with people you may not know well.

Verse 8 adds the thought that by supporting God's workers, we actually become "fellow workers" of the truth. That means that when we invest in missionaries in China, Romania, Honduras, we may be doing more than we realize. When we pray for them, write to them, give to support their work, and share news of what they are doing for the kingdom of God, in a true sense we become partners in their work even though they are on the other side of the world.

Gaius was that kind of man. He welcomed God's workers into his home, supported them, and sent them on their way so they could preach in other places. In so doing, he became a "fellow worker" with them and shared in their victories for the Lord. He also gave himself the chance to see vivid examples of Christ's love at work through these dedicated servants. He gave himself a front-row seat to something worth imitating.

We Are to Imitate Good, Not Evil

We live in a world of tremendous diversity. Nowhere is that more true than in the myriad expressions of Christian faith. While some may not differ much on basics of the faith, within the finer points there is tremendous disagreement. The writer of 3 John reminds us that, eventually, Christian charity and character are tests to which all must submit. We are measured by a standard of the "truth"—the goodness and life of Christ as modeled for us and placed in our lives even now by God's Spirit.

He tells us to imitate "good" and not evil. There are two references to characters here. One is Diotrephes. A man in Pastor H. A. Ironside's church always tried to run the board meetings. If Ironside agreed with him, everything went well, but when he disagreed, he received a harsh letter from the man, who sarcastically addressed him as "Dear Diotrephes." Actually, the board member deserved the title, not Ironside, who was known for his graciousness (Stedman, 1989). Throughout the epistles of John we are reminded that Diotrephes is an opposing force to the good that is identified with Christ's "truth." He is a confusing foe because he presents himself as one of the "followers" and would pretend to teach and lead. I'm sure he was dynamic and impressive. Handsome. Probably loud and quick to speak up. Popular. Intriguing.

What does Diotrephes do that is so bad? He refuses hospitality to the Christian "brethren" sent by John. He openly speaks evil of John. These things are bad enough within the early Christian movement, but he also puts out of the church those who try to be hospitable to people who come in Christ's truth. John also says Diotrephes "puts himself first above others." There are apparently other offenses, and these letters seem to lean on previous and commonly known issues of character. As often happens, people followed Diotrephes. They imitated him as a way of doing church!

My belief is that there's far too much more of a "Diotrephean" spirit in the household of God than we may like to think. There is a widely circulated story about the great Baptist scholar A. T. Robertson. As the tale goes, Robertson once wrote a scholarly article on Diotrephes for a denominational paper. The editor told him later that, after the article was published, twenty-five deacons from various churches wrote to cancel their subscriptions. They did so in protest, to show their resentment against being personally attacked! We may laugh that off, but the truth is that many of us can testify, through painful personal experience, what a terrible trial it is when the household of God falls under the control of a church member with a domineering spirit. Such modern-day Diotrepheses may be able to convince themselves that they're doing the Lord's work, but those of us who have seen them in action know that they actually hinder and damage the work of God.

But another player here is Demetrius. Demetrius is different from Diotrephes. His reputation seems not only solid, but he has another thing that John believes counts—what he calls "testimony from the truth itself." That is, when held up to the gospel teachings (or "truth") of Christ's goodness, Demetrius's life stands as a loving example. Under the scrutiny of this testimony from the truth, his substance holds up. The good news of Christ is lived noticeably through him, rather than that gospel becoming a convicting argument against his character. Demetrius lived by attitudes of faith and love. He didn't merely believe them, didn't only preach them, and didn't just judge others by them. He was *known by* these qualities!

What Is the Benchmark?

Testimony from "everyone" is good to a point. To some degree, we all long to be liked and accepted. There is nothing wrong with that. I would even say that more often than not, the crowd gets it right. I prefer to be liked by more people rather than by fewer. The trouble is that the "testimony of everyone," the *consensus ominum*, can be wrong! As much as we all love our country's freedoms founded on majority rule—and even our church governance—we have to admit that sometimes the group *can* get it wrong! We remember the crowd crying out for Barabbas at the expense of Christ hanging on the cross, or Christ himself rebuking the disciples when he said, "suffer the little children to come unto me" (Luke 23:18; Matt 19:14).

John raises for us the character standard of the "truth itself" to which our lives as Christians are compared. His words will not just help us fulfill individual fidelity to Christ; living by these words will benefit the entire fellowship of believers. Maybe most of the people around us will be the better for our healthy living, too. And his instruction is simply profound—imitate what is good! That which holds up well in comparison with our Lord is living by the truth. Choose for your living what will stand the test of time. Live by values that are in keeping with God's purposes for life, rather than in keeping with human purposes for life.

As we try to figure out what to do with this passage, I think there's a problem for some of us. We have three church members in this story. Two of them are worthy of being imitated, and the Elder tells locals to do exactly that. But the third one is not worthy of being held up as a role model. He actually represents evil, or certainly an opposing faith stance. That causes some of us trouble. I know that on our worst days, we all are capable of acting like the one we are warned against.

But there are people, Christians, whose behavior is frequently not exemplary. Not all characters influence us in a positive direction with regard to our own character. Today, I think 3 John has a clear word for us—to imitate what is good and not imitate what is not good. Here's the problem: We have to be willing to allow ourselves to look at one another and say, "That does not represent Christ to me, and I won't go along with it. That fellow Christian does nothing to make me want to be a better person. But this one does. That's a little closer to Christ personified. I'll step away from his patterns and keep a closer eye on how she lives."

Not all things that say Christian and read Christian and sound Christian are going to lead us to Christ! That means we have to know what we believe. We have to think about our faith. We have to work at our faith in order to know what we believe. "Beloved, do not imitate what is evil, but what is good. He who does good is of God, but he who does evil has not seen God."

A minister of music was fine-tuning the way his choir would sing an important piece of literature. He was showing the choir a technique for producing the best possible sound. Old habits were difficult for the singers to overcome, and he continued searching for a clear way to unlock their understanding. He modeled the way they should sing the piece, and he played a recording of a group performing the piece exactly the same way. Then he observed, "Good singing is, in part, imitating other good singers!" And so it is.

One dad said it this way: "My son is four years old. If I want to teach him something, I usually have to show him how to do it. If it is difficult, I will show him again and again. But soon he will imitate me and can do it by himself. We have a difficult time now, though, because my son is getting older. He used to have few models to imitate. My wife, myself, Grandma, and Grandpa. But now he has many models. Some are good—Christian friends, teachers, good television programs. But some are not so good. Now he brings home strange words, imitating his friends. Sometimes he does things that are strange. The other day he started to pull down his pants and sing a silly song. I found out that he was imitating something he had seen on TV."

Part of growing up is learning who to imitate and who not to imitate. The Christian life is the same way. The Apostle Paul said, "Imitate me, as I imitate Christ" (1 Cor 11:1). Like that little boy, if we want to learn how to live our lives for Christ, we need a practical model to follow. We can listen to someone talk about living as Christ and not quite understand, but if we see someone doing it, then we can do so too.

God put this letter in the Bible perhaps mostly to show us who to imitate and who not to imitate. But one thing we struggle with is admitting that we should imitate anybody at all, and the truth is that everybody in God's kingdom might not be worthy of imitating. Still, I think in the core of our souls we know these things to be true.

Some of you give tremendous amounts of time and energy to God's kingdom, including through the local church. We should imitate you. Some take great lengths to care for fellow believers in their churches who have reached a point in life where they depend upon others. We should imitate you. So many participate faithfully in the stewardship giving that keeps the church vital and healthy in God's kingdom. We should imitate you. Some of you believe that the church is central to your practice of faith in community, just as believers did in the early church of the New Testament. We should imitate you. Some of you seem to have God's spirit about how to be sensitive to what is going on in the lives of hurting people around you, and 3 John says that in Jesus' name we should most certainly imitate you. For these are the things on which God's kingdom is built!

1. Whom have you imitated in your lifetime? (heroes, sports figures, TV/movie characters, others)

_____

_____

_____

_____

2. Although you probably didn't consider the matter back then, how did you choose whom you imitated?

_____

_____

_____

_____

3. What can we learn from role-playing and imitation as children?

_____

_____

_____

_____

4. What healthy or unhealthy developments happen to cause adults to shy away from imitation? Or, if you believe we don't stop imitating, then why do we hesitate to admit that we mimic others?

_____

_____

_____

_____

5. How would you describe the power of good role models against instructive words we might read or hear? Would you say you learn easier from watching others or from reading/hearing?

_____

_____

_____

_____

6. Much of the content in John's epistles is in reaction to "false teachers." When the book, person, writing, or song says it is "Christian," how might you know whether it truly is? How might you know that the content does *not* represent Christ?

_____

_____

_____

_____

7. Why do we struggle so much to admit that not all of those in God's kingdom might be worthy of imitation?

_____

_____

_____

_____

8. In this chapter, we hear, "Live by values that are in keeping with God's purposes for life, rather than in keeping with human purposes for life." How would you sum up some of the values that reflect God?

_____

_____

_____

_____

Bibliography

Barker, Glen W. *1, 2, 3 John*. The Expositor's Bible Commentary. Volume 12. Grand Rapids: Zondervan, 1981.

Erdman, Charles R. *The General Epistles*. Commentaries on the New Testament. Philadelphia: Westminster Press, 1929.

Hollingsworth, James N. Doctoral seminar discussion. Atlanta: McAfee School of Theology, 2004.

Johnson, Earl S., Jr. *James, 1st and 2nd Peter, 1st, 2nd, and 3rd John and Jude*. Basic Bible Commentary. Nashville: Abingdon Press, 1988.

Lewis Institute, C. S. Biographical entry on website. http://www.cslewisinstitute.org/cslewis/index.htm.

Marshall, Peter, and David Manuel. *The Light and the Glory*. Ada MI: Fleming H. Revell Company, 1977.

McCullar, Michael. *Sessions with James*. Macon GA: Smyth & Helwys Publishing, 2001.

McDowell, Edward. *1-2-3 John*. Volume 12. Nashville: Broadman Bible Commentary, 1972.

Smalley, Stephen S. *1, 2, 3 John*. Word Biblical Commentary. Volume 51. Nashville: Thomas Nelson Publishers, 1984.

Smith, D. Moody. *1, 2, 3 John*. Interpretation Commentary. Louisville: Westminster/John Knox Press, 1991.

Stedman, Ray. "The Church that Lost Its Love, Revelation 1:19–2:7." Web-based sermon, 12 November 1989. Message 2, catalog 4190. Palo Alto: Discovery Publishing.

Summers, Ray. *Jude*. Volume 12. Nashville: Broadman Bible Commentary, 1972.

Wilder, Amos N., and Paul W. Hoon. *The First, Second, and Third Epistles of John*. The Interpreter's Bible Commentary. Nashville: Abingdon Press, 1957.